HOW TO EARN
MORE MONEY
FROM YOUR CRAFTS

HOW TO EARN MORE MONEY FROM YOUR CRAFTS

MERLE E. DOWD

Doubleday & Company, Inc., Garden City, New York   1976

Library of Congress Cataloging in Publication Data

Dowd, Merle E
  How to earn more money from your crafts.

  Includes index.
    1. Handicraft—Marketing.   I. Title.
HD2341.D68   381'.45'7455
ISBN 0-385-07715-7
Library of Congress Catalog Card Number 75-6156

Dedicated to
Barbara Brabec of *ARTISAN CRAFTS*,
a tireless worker for better
marketing by craftsmen

CONTENTS

HOW CRAFTSMEN CAN BENEFIT
FROM THIS BOOK

Crafts of all kinds have come of age with a resounding boom. Jewelry, stitchery, macramé, flowercraft, weedcraft, driftwood polishing and carving, woodworking, glass blowing, candlecraft—the list is practically endless. Handcrafted products are turning up for sale in gift shops, in hospital auxiliary bazaars, in galleries, and on street corners. Classes in crafts, with or without credit, are among the most popular courses offered at community colleges or as part of high school adult education evening programs.

Craft books, either the how-to variety or the beautifully produced coffee-table volumes, proliferate without apparent end. Older books with a maximum of words and a minimum of drawings and photos are being replaced by books crammed with detailed how-to drawings and exciting photographs. *Lapidary Journal*, a specialized magazine catering to gemstone hunters, polishers, cutters, and handcraft jewelers, sells 75,000 copies of craft books each year.

Specialized magazines cater to the interests of those interested in specific crafts. Established magazines, such as *Craft Horizons*, are growing bigger as the desire for craft information and materials continues to grow.

Craft fairs and festivals, probably the greatest barometer of interest in crafts, feature arts and crafts on weekends in communities all across the land. In a carnival atmosphere, summer fairs offer a great outpouring of creative endeavor in multiple media. "Artists in Action" draw wanderers to watch a painter finishing a portrait in his sidewalk studio; a woodcarver piling cedar chips underfoot as he roughs out a door-high totemlike figure; a silversmith forging sterling for a choker; a potter firing glaze in a thundering gas-fired furnace.

Many reasons are advanced to account for the burgeoning interest in handcrafts. More disposable income figures as one big factor. Crafts don't qualify as necessities by any stretch of the definition. A flood of handcrafts from cottage industries out of foreign lands prompted part of this growth.

Probably the major reason behind the explosion of handcrafts is the growing revolt against "look-alikes." Young people have rushed to establish their own individuality. In an era of mass production, the one-of-a-kind ring, ceramic lamp base, oil painting, stitchery wall hanging—or any of the other multitude of crafts—restates the identity of two persons, the craftsman and the buyer. Craftsmen dig in or dabble in crafts to express their own individuality. Buyers of crafts express their own individuality through the items they purchase.

Your Opportunity to Profit

The widening interest in crafts affords a new and higher plateau of opportunity for the producing craftsman. There are almost as many ways to profit from this new-found and exploding interest in crafts as there are crafts. Simply producing craft products and selling them has always been the direct approach. Yet marketing and production can be—*must be*—tied closely together to achieve the most profitable mix.

Improving the profitability of craftsmen's activities is the single major thrust of this book. It aims to help you improve your income by increasing the net dollar return for each hour you spend at your bench, hopefully without extracting the fun—a major challenge, to be sure.

Potentially more profitable than producing and selling crafts is capitalizing your know-how; that is, marketing your hard-won experience and creative expertise. Writing about your crafts, teaching your crafts to others, selling special equipment you've developed to simplify craft techniques or to reduce the cost, marketing materials, or selling kits that introduce newcomers to the enjoyment of crafts can be enormously profitable—and your craft know-how is the key.

Three levels of interest can be identified among craftsmen:

Some craftsmen sell their creations to friends and neighbors for just enough cash to finance the purchase of more materials or equipment. Their primary interest relates not to earning an income but to practicing their craft as a hobby on a pay-as-they-go basis. These craftsmen gain what economists call "psychic income" from their activities. They care little about the dollar return per hour of effort expended, particularly during early learning stages. Some of the ideas in this book will interest these hobbyists, because they can turn over their craftwork quicker and get on with the pleasurable task of converting more materials into finished products and extending their expertise.

Part-time craftsmen comprise by far the greatest number of serious producers. They remain part-timers for one overriding reason: They can't make a living pursuing their craft full time. Many reasons account for this recognized fact of life. But the main reason behind their part-time status relates to their lack of interest or abilities in marketing. As creative individuals they ply their pleasurable activity and accept whatever meager return they can earn without recognizing the marketing potential of their craft activities.

Such part-timers look at other creative pursuits to find company among struggling, underpaid, and exploited creative people throughout a community. Musicians, even those of symphony orchestra status, usually supplement their earnings by teaching or moonlighting. Writers compete with amateurs who willingly supply manuscripts to publishers for little more than a byline. Television producers pay less for the creative content of television shows than for any other element in productions that frequently are billed to sponsors for hundreds of thousands of dollars. Painters, sculptors, composers, and most of the other creative specialists supplement their artistry with an income-producing sideline or full-time job.

Finally, at the top are those creative individuals who function full time as professional craftsmen and earn a respectable income from their effort and talent. Creative craftsmen reach this pinnacle through their individual work and talent or as the guiding genius of an organization that utilizes effective marketing. In every community there are a few of these full-timers. They sell their crafts. They teach. They lecture for significant fees or earn cash as honorariums for judging or consulting. One key to their lofty position is a *name*—a reputation carefully nourished through a variety of promotion activities.

Some of the most successful craftsmen-entrepreneurs sell unique products, market their know-how through a functioning distribution system, or cater to the needs of other craftsmen.

Among these successful entrepreneurs runs a common thread that accounts for much of their success. A candlemaker so intent on creating a shadowy picture through the sides of a cube as the center burns that he throws out 90 per cent of his products makes a good living from the sales of that 10 per cent that meet his standards.

A jewelry metal crafter translates his skill into two marketable products—innovative special tools that simplify many of the difficult techniques in jewelry crafting and classes that feature intense instruction where students produce jewelry they can be proud to wear after only two hours of instruction.

A weaver uses only the authentic colors of wool as grown on the sheep and spins every hank of yarn that goes into her products. A macramé artist dyes all of her own thread and yarn to produce exotic color combinations available nowhere else.

Common among these individual craftsmen is the *quality of uniqueness.* Whether that uniqueness results from uncommon materials, innovative tooling or teaching methodology, or design, the quality of that uniqueness sets these craftsmen apart. And they prosper accordingly.

As you'll see from the following chapters, making money from your craft calls for dedication to design and creativity—plus production. There is no short cut for the producing craftsman to cash in without spending hours and hours at his bench. At some fork in the road you must decide whether to produce numbers of similar pieces or continue to produce one-of-a-kind creations. Producing a number of similar pieces based on a common design can be particularly profitable, but routine production can also degenerate into work by the hour. Developing new designs for each product offers fun and releases the full flow of creativity. Such a route may also lead to meager earnings unless the designer achieves a reputation that increases the market value of each creation.

Craftsmen can pursue both routes successfully. Individually successful craftsmen couple both activities—continuing to produce creative designs that gain a reputation in the shows and galleries while turning out many similar pieces for sale.

"Good taste is a minority opinion"—or so goes one myth circulating among craftsmen. Yet people, in general, have exhibited surprisingly consistent good taste over the years. What appears to be *avant garde* or "in" often turns out later to have been a fad. Generally, good taste leads to profits in the market place. There is no need for the producing craftsman to downgrade his artistry or creativity by attempting to reach a so-called popular level of taste to achieve volume sales. Other alternatives, as detailed in these chapters, can be exploited to develop volume sales for the craftsman who can produce a continuing flow of creative and distinctive craft products.

Not all crafts benefit equally from exposure and marketing. Pottery sells because it can be utilitarian. Ceramic sculpture also sells even though a product cannot be used in the kitchen or patio. Sculpture may be decorative, inspiring, or functional—or all three. Whatever the end result, pottery and ceramics enjoy one indigenous benefit—few people can get into pottery without some substantial investment in time and equipment. So, potters and ceramicists continue to sell their works and their know-how.

Contrast ceramics with a craft like macramé, knitting, or dry weed arranging. People dabble with macramé on a do-it-yourself basis. The creative macramé craftsman therefore pursues another route to making money—teaching, selling materials, or packaging kits with instructions for the do-it-yourselfer. Further, the outstanding macramé craftsman writes a book on the art and profits from singular and unique designs displayed as examples in the book.

One of the simplest crafts to learn offers "instant gratification" by producing plastic leaves and petals. A formed wire is dipped into a liquid plastic that forms a surface between the wires and dries as a flexible film. This popular craft can be learned in a single afternoon. New designs and continued development of the craft offer little challenge to the serious craftsman. Yet, one craftsman-entrepreneur has literally earned a small fortune supplying kits of materials and instructions by mail to beginner craftsmen all over the world.

How much can craftsmen earn? Attempting a simple answer to such a general question would be extreme folly. The craftsman with a world-wide reputation earns as much as the writer of a best seller.

But many, many lesser talents subsist on a meager income. How much you can earn depends on your craft, your production rate, your marketing savvy, how well you promote yourself, and how effectively you integrate proved business practices and marketing know-how with your craft creativity. Only you can put all the pieces together. Helping you pull the pieces together and earn more of the cash you believe you are entitled to—that's the objective of this book.

For starters:

You can earn more than you have been earning.

You can learn from the successes and failures of others.

You can benefit from a vast background of experience without retracing the steps of the many who have gone before.

You can learn marketing—the complement of your craft—and use marketing techniques, strategy, and know-how to EARN MORE MONEY FROM YOUR CRAFTS.

HOW TO EARN
MORE MONEY
FROM YOUR CRAFTS

Chapter 1

MARKETING YOUR CRAFTS
AND KNOW-HOW

Marketing of crafts differs only in detail from marketing any other product. But successful, full-time producing-teaching craftsmen recognize that the "better mousetrap" approach to marketing no longer works.

Marketing involves advertising, selecting and developing channels of distribution, pricing, promotion—and selling. When you begin to think about making more money from your crafts, you begin to think about marketing. As you think about selling, examine the marketplace. See how it functions whatever the product—crafts, teaching or developing material and tools for other craftsmen.

You can carve a place for yourself in this market by promoting yourself and your products—by putting your crafts on a business basis. Take the example of Bill Garrison, a master jewelry craftsman and designer with a broad outlook on craft markets.

HANDCRAFTS, USA represents his plan to help American craftsmen combat imported handcrafts. For the craftsman more interested in producing than diluting his efforts in marketing attempts, HANDCRAFTS, USA offers a co-operative sales plan and a distribution network through direct-mail selling to shops, galleries, and craft fairs. Instead of selling on consignment, craftsmen set their own wholesale price. Terms to dealers are "Cash in Advance," a marked contrast to consignment selling (see Chapter 5). Jewelry, only one of the craft lines being sold, may be one-of-a-kind originals, limited editions, or semiproduction pieces. Many of the crafts being offered for sale come from Garrison's students.

Goods, including crafts, are not bought in today's market—they are sold! As a marketer, you must "move the goods." Begin by asking yourself these questions:

❖ How is my craft different from all the other crafts competing for buyers' dollars? For example, if your craft is jewelry, are your designs unique? Do they use different materials? Different construction?

❖ Why are my designs important?

❖ Who buys craft products like mine?

❖ Why do they buy them?

❖ How will my products compete for attention?

❖ Are my crafts priced competitively?

All of these questions impact your position in the marketplace because handcrafts fall into the "luxury" market. People buy crafts because they like them, not because they are essential for day-to-day living. Most crafts are decorative rather than useful. Some, such as pottery, can be both. Crafts are bought largely on impulse.

Underlying much of the burgeoning interest in crafts among noncraftsmen is the desire to be different, to be distinctive—to be considered a unique individual. People buy crafts to achieve individual distinction by acquiring items that reflect their own highly individual taste. When a woman selects a pair of dangling handcrafted earrings, she knows they are unique. The design may be similar to others, but her earrings are handcrafted—not stamped out by machine. By buying handcrafts, she votes against depersonalization in the machine age. She exercises her distinction as an authentic individual by selecting and wearing an original design or exhibiting crafts in other media to reflect her taste.

One jeweler relates how she learned about individualized crafts. "A lady brought in two small opals, souvenirs of a trip to Australia. They were brilliant opals, and I could tell she had endowed them with sentimental memories of her trip. She wanted the opals crafted into earrings, uniquely designed and executed in eighteen karat gold. I spent too much time on them, but I wanted to turn out a superb job. When I finished, they were flawless; I was proud of them. But when the lady came to pick them up, she refused them. 'They are too perfect,' she remarked, a little annoyed. 'If I had wanted a perfect job, I could have taken them any number of places. I wanted *handcrafted* earrings.' Somewhat deflated, I reworked the pair of earrings, leaving prongs slightly askew with a bit of metal not removed at the joints. Slight differences distinguished one from the other. On second examination, the lady was delighted. The earrings were not only uniquely styled, they were handcrafted—and looked it. Even a casual examination showed they were not machine made."

When you market jewelry or any other craft product, you sell distinction through individual, unique styling.

Get Involved in Marketing

As a producing craftsman you design and produce goods for sale. You will already have discovered how much easier and more satisfying it is to design, experiment, and work at your craft than it is to sell what you make. Or you may find, as one craftsman relates it, "I get a million dollars in oohs and ahhs, but only $1.98 in cash."

To "move the goods," you must initiate action. Learn about marketing from all the sources in the following chapters—by talking with other craftsmen and by following the marketing activities of others. Then, dive in. You can expect to make mistakes. Not all of your products will sell. Some will net you a greater return on your efforts than others. But once you begin and carry through, you build on experience.

Consider, for example, the different channels of distribution. You might sell your goods directly to buyers. Or you could develop wholesale or consignment outlets through personal selling or by mail. Another option is an intermediary, such as HANDCRAFTS, USA, one of the associations of craftsmen, or an agent. Associations help by spreading the marketing load among many participating craftsmen.

One of the most successful associations is the Alaska Native Arts-Crafts Cooperative Association, Inc., known as ANAC. The association is owned and directed by natives representing all sections of Alaska—Eskimos, Indians, and Aleuts. Under manager Don Burrus, recently retired, ANAC grew until sales volume at wholesale averaged $150,000 a year. ANAC is a nonprofit co-operative that sells through a retail store in Juneau and through a catalogue it issues to dealers throughout the United States. Alaskan crafts include grass baskets, drawings on animal skins, ceremonial masks carved from wood and whalebone, totems, jewelry, and the unique ivory carvings that unmistakably mark the pieces as Alaskan. Demand for ANAC crafts now far exceeds the supply available from Alaskan craftsmen even though prices are high enough to discourage "bauble buyers."

Alaskan crafts move through ANAC when they would not otherwise because the carvers and painters live in remote villages. Only by banding together could they offer a variety of goods through an attractive catalogue to shops in New York, Florida, and the other states in the "lower forty-eight." Local associations may operate a shop under a nonprofit corporate arrangement. To make it happen, a group of interested craftsmen become involved in "doing their own thing." Northwest Craft Center in Seattle, Washington, functions as a consignment shop under the direction of a board of five involved craftsmen. Hundreds of craftsmen sell their products to visitors attracted to the Seattle Center, site of the Seattle World's Fair in 1962.

A Show of Hands operates as a co-operative in New York City with a fluctuating membership of around forty craftsmen. When A Show of Hands opened its new shop on Broadway, co-operative members paid a one-time fee of $50 to join plus $12 each month as a hanging fee to cover minimum exhibition costs. Sales are on consignment with the shop taking 25 per cent of the gross to cover operations. Members must contribute eight hours of work each month with the jobs parceled out according to interests and skills—bookkeeping, publicity, decoration—plus sales. A selection committee passes on the acceptability of crafts to be exhibited for sale in the shop. Such a sharing of interest, labor, and costs makes far more sense for many craftsmen than attempting to operate an individual shop (see Chapter 6).

Involved craftsmen in the quiet fishing village of Gig Harbor, Washington, banded together to promote the area into an internationally known arts and crafts center. Galleries and co-operative shops offer local crafts to visitors winter and summer. Through community action and craftsmen involvement, crafts sell in a quiet, creative environment highlighted by special shows, previews, receptions, and fairs that bring customers face to face with craftsmen.

Summer arts and crafts fairs offer an ideal opportunity for craftsmen to become involved, to test the market for their goods, and to move months of production into customers' hands. Summer fairs are fun times when craftsmen take orders for custom pieces while educating the public on the place of handcrafts and art in today's often depersonalized world.

Crafts as a Business

Making money from creative crafts can be frustrating due to a number of inherent constraints. Competition between serious craftsmen and hobbyists tends to deflate prices. Hobbyists may sell their crafts for only enough cash to replace materials used or to buy equipment. They enjoy the creative activity and couldn't care less about the money. Many dedicated hobbyists turn out exquisite work. They may spend painstaking hours on individual pieces without considering their time as a cost in the value of the product.

The producing craftsman ignores these talented hobbyists at his peril, for they remain a major factor in local craft markets. The producing craftsman competes by offering consistent quality, on-time delivery, a businesslike approach in dealing with shops and galleries, and a sensible pricing policy (see Chapter 3). The producing craftsman also distinguishes his work by promoting himself, designing distinctively styled pieces, and offering a greater variety and volume of goods for sale than the hobbyist.

As a business, handcrafts suffer two other handicaps:

First, craftsmen are plentiful because there are few limitations on entry and a relatively minor capital investment is required. Further, the fun of participating in crafts is heavily promoted through magazines, books, and classes. Making money from your craft requires dedication and serious work. As a producing, marketing craftsman, you can excel by developing unique products and marketing them through a variety of channels.

For an unusual marketing approach consider the man who sells paintings door to door. His wife paints the pictures in watercolor and oil. He sells them for an average of $50 each. Selling door to door, probably the toughest kind of cold-call selling, yields the couple an average gross of five hundred dollars a week. An unusual approach? Yes—but quite remunerative.

The market for arts and crafts is all around you if you are smart enough to reach for it. As a producing craftsman, your job is to divert a small part of your creativity into marketing. Find new, unique, and profitable ways of tapping the market for your crafts.

Direct selling, confronting the public with goods for sale, still works. For example, rather than try to entice potential buyers into shops or galleries, enterprising craftsmen hawk their wares on New York and San Francisco streets—to the dismay of established business. Police have put many sidewalk businesses off the street, but they pop up in other places where they can show their crafts to the public—in a farmer's market, a storefront downtown, or a county fair. Marketing your crafts can become an engaging activity if you rise to the challenge. If the income from crafts becomes important to your life style, plan to spend time and effort learning marketing strategy.

The second major constraint is how much your two hands can produce. The unique quality of handcrafts depends, of course, on *hand* work. Skilled craftsmen run out of time when producing handcrafts for sale in competition with imports. Cottage industries abound in countries where labor is cheap—Mexico, Hong Kong, Haiti, and others. As a producing craftsman, you will find shortcuts for producing more salable items to increase your take-home pay per hour. Casting jewelry uses machine methods to increase production. Molding candles speeds one operation. However, machine methods or shortcuts must retain the look and design effects of handwork to assure their sale to customers looking for distinctive crafts.

Creations vs. Production

Designer craftsmen look askance at the craftsman who turns out many similar "look-alikes." You may be torn between the desire for artistic acclaim and an income from your craft production. Designs that win show awards appeal to a different level of taste than crafts produced for sale at prices most customers can afford. There's a reason for this difference. Designer craftsmen competing for awards know they will be judged by peers with *avant-garde* tastes. Judges will recognize truly original designs from run-of-the-mill crafts because of their broad and intensive familiarity with what has been produced already. Judges look intently for designs that are new and creative. Yet, while craft creations with a high design content competently crafted may win awards, they often fall flat in the marketplace.

The shrewd, marketing-oriented craftsman plays both games. He enters competitions and contests with innovative creations that win awards to help build his reputation. A name gained competitively can be valuable as an opening wedge for gallery shows and publicity. Creations can be quickly priced out of the general market because potential buyers are few and creations scarce. Some outstanding craftsmen excel in this lofty market sustained by rarity and exclusive design. They are the elite. Producing craftsmen offer a balance—truly creative designs to gain a name recognized by the public and goods produced in volume for sale at prices a broad segment of the public can appreciate and afford.

Marketing is the broad term that encompasses all activities related to moving crafts from producer to customer. Marketing means more than selling. Marketing involves pricing, promotion, distribution, and producing with an eye on the market. The following chapters tackle each of these important marketing functions in turn along with alternatives. Case histories of craftsmen who continue to earn money from their crafts prove that marketing pays off handsomely for those who become involved. Once you embrace the essential elements of marketing and consider selling as only one important function, you too can "earn more money from your crafts."

Chapter 2

PROMOTING YOURSELF

AND YOUR CRAFTS

Crafts are generating increasing interest and excitement in the marketplace. Witness the crowds that flock to weekend arts and crafts fairs to see craftsmen in action and to buy craft products. People come for another reason too, for most individuals recognize an inner need to be creative, to make something with their own hands, and to dream a little. You can tap these wellsprings of interest in crafts to achieve a number of your own objectives—

❖ Wider visibility for your own, unique accomplishments as an individual and producing craftsman.

❖ Greater sales potential as more people know and understand your craft expressions.

❖ Greater opportunity for merchandising lessons, materials, and tools.

The days of "hiding your light under a bushel" are long gone. To make money from your craft—by whatever avenue you choose and regardless of the media—people must know you. If you learn to promote yourself with the same creativity as you exhibit in your crafts, your reputation will blossom. When people hear about you, see and appreciate your craftwork, and recognize your unique designs and creativity, profits from your crafts will follow as inexorably as day follows night.

Publicity, promotion, and advertising all aim to help people learn about you. Since advertising costs you money, consider it last. Concentrate on publicity and promotion as no-cost or low-cost avenues for getting your name before the public. What's the difference between publicity and promotion? Both aim at getting people to know you. If there is a difference, it's that promotion includes sales brochures, reduced price sales (your craft seconds, for example), becoming a craftsman in action, direct mail solicitation, or one of the other sales activities. Publicity, on the other hand, is aimed at letting people know who you are and what you do indirectly. Sales of your product, lessons, or materials and equipment follow later, possibly aided by direct sales promotion. When you appear at a preview of your work in a gallery, you are promoting your products. When a newspaper article appears heralding the opening of your one-man show at the XYZ Gallery—that's publicity for you.

You gain maximum advantage from publicity and promotion only when you actively participate. Look around at your craftsmen friends objectively. Those who are well known were their own best press agents. You can hire someone to take photographs or possibly write up news releases, but only you know what you are doing. Only you know why your craft expressions are important. Tune in—become alert to the possibilities of publicity and promotion. Understand that a flair for the dramatic or a bit of "show business" makes the difference between whether or not you appear on TV or are featured in a newspaper. For example—

Barry Houlihan appears at southeastern arts and crafts fairs in a broad-brimmed tropical straw hat to protect his fair skin from the sun. He wears a bright red shirt you can see a block away. Strollers are drawn to his stand by the ringing sounds of metal on metal as he forges pieces for his welded sculptures. He operates with a flourish, confidently directing the hissing torch to join hot metal into suggestive figures. Further, he talks as he works to explain the different steps in creating a table-size or floor-height figure.

"Indian John" Gibbons is a joy to watch as he hacks away rough chunks of dry cedar while carving a totem. Or he whangs away with mallet and chisel. Chips cascade around the area, as he works fast. Some visitors watch for hours as the primitive figures emerge under the skilled woodcarver's deft strokes. And he makes it look so simple!

These craftsmen are actors too. By promoting themselves, they sell their skill and their crafts. Every craftsman can add a little "show biz" to his or her act at craft fairs, on the women's club lecture circuit, and in teaching. Demonstrations and teaching can be exciting. Make them interesting and people will remember you and your work. When your name on a craft product strikes a familiar chord with a potential buyer—the sale is half made. Visibility definitely pays off in the marketplace.

Publicity challenges you to a game of wits. With advertising, you can control the time, place, and content. Publicity demands greater skill in devising a program that will catch the interest of an editor or program director. To achieve visibility through publicity, you must offer something worthwhile to the reader or viewer. Examine publicity possibilities from the viewpoint of the reader or viewer. You may wish to publicize some facet of your work, but unless that idea is new and different enough to generate interest, newspapers, radio, or TV media will not be interested. Here is where your creativity plays such an important role. For example—

Jeff Robson worked in a variety of media—one-of-a-kind lamps, carved furniture, wall hangings in wood and metal, and wire jewelry, plus painting and sketching in charcoal. Just for fun, he began teaching junior-high boys and girls how to fashion simple wire jewelry at his combination shop-gallery. It started with a young girl who showed up after school at the alley doorway of his studio. She asked simply, "Can I watch?" Jeff invited her in and asked if she would like to play with wire and pliers. After only one session, the girl took away a pair of simple earrings formed in polished copper wire—eyes ablaze with excitement.

The next day she brought a friend. Soon, from four to eight boys and girls were busily working with wire and pliers around the alley doorway to Jeff's shop. Jeff told a friend of a city councilman about the kids. The councilman promptly told a reporter, who dropped by the impromptu classes for a look. He was intrigued by Jeff's teaching a creative activity in a manner that absorbed the young people's interest.

The outcome was a feature-length article in the Sunday magazine complete with photos. Along with Jeff's teaching activities, the story told about his studio-gallery and showed photos of individual wire jewelry pieces crafted by the students, along with directions for finding his out-of-the-way location. Immediately and for months later visitors, who would otherwise have never known of Jeff Robson's gallery, dropped in to browse and buy. Further, Jeff was invited to display his work at other galleries, and his reputation began gathering luster rapidly. Jeff was canny enough to recognize the benefits of publicity. By planting the lead, he developed his publicity break. You can make your own breaks by providing newsworthy hooks to hang a story on. Here's how—

Craft Fairs and Exhibitions

Opportunities abound for exhibiting and selling your crafts at the summer arts and crafts fairs (see Chapter 4). Summer festivals have become so popular they are expanding into the fall and pre-Christmas season. Rather than simply display your crafts, develop your "craftsman in action" plan whatever the season. If you are a potter, rig up a portable wheel and take your clay and glazes along to demonstrate how you craft your wares. Wood carving and jewelry crafting offer similar opportunities for demonstration. Flowercraft is easily demonstrated and will attract more interest than a simple display of finished flowers and materials. As a craftsman in action you draw more than interest from passersby—you open the door to advance publicity.

Your first step is to contact the publicity chairman of the fair. You can bet he or she will be looking for photo opportunities to help promote the fair. Any publicity chairman worth his title will have access to the press and television where you, as an individual, might not.

Take the initiative and call the publicity chairman for an appointment. Then, do your homework in preparation for your presentation. Collect photos showing you in action. Don't rely on quick snapshots. Ask one of your photographer friends to take professional photos of you and representative samples of your craft. Take along some of your craft products if they are small. Sell yourself and your craft to the publicity chairman as a craftsman who will attract visitors to the fair. Brainstorm ideas for promotion with the chairman—such as an interview with a local newspaper writer, demonstrating your craft on television, or performing at a shopping center under the fair's banner. The publicity chairman will generate a number of ideas if he is doing his job. Publicity chairmen experience a number of difficulties in doing their job. When you offer to help, you make their job easier—and you gain the visibility that helps build your reputation.

Juried craft fairs sponsored by nonprofit organizations of craftsmen offer the best opportunities for publicity. Media understand the difference between a co-operative effort by craftsmen and a show that exploits any craftsman willing to buy booth space. Avoid the shows where you must buy your way in. Concentrate instead on those fairs where quality craftsmanship and design earn you a spot in the program through competition. Association with your peers elevates your opportunities for publicity—and sales.

Opportunities for Publicity in Print

Newspapers, magazines, television, radio, and groups offer almost inexhaustible opportunities for publicity when you understand the rules and the mutual benefits. Let's look at each media in turn—

Newspaper—Remember, first and foremost, that a newspaper operates for profit. By publishing news, features, and information of interest to the community, newspapers draw readership. A newspaper makes its money by selling advertisements to merchants and others interested in communicating with readers. A newspaper is not a quasi-public institution to mold community character or promote individuals like yourself. Free space in a newspaper for publicity is scarce. You can appreciate its worth by pricing advertising space. At $1 to $15 a column inch you can see how much the space for a feature with a photograph costs the paper. You compete with organizations and individuals for access to this space by developing such an interesting story about yourself and your craft that editors will feel compelled to pass it along to readers. Jeff Robson's story appealed to readers because he offered a human interest story—a program for teaching disadvantaged children a new craft skill.

Publicizing events calls for a specific technique. Suppose your crafts are to be exhibited in a gallery kicked off by a preview. You'll want to co-operate with the gallery owner in developing a publicity release. Build your story around the five "w's"—who, what, why, when, and where. If possible, work these five "w's" into the lead paragraph of your story. For example—

Gaylord Hines opens a one-man show of his culinary pottery at the Cue Gallery, 114 South Bonney, with a preview beginning at 4 P.M. on Sunday, October 12. Hines's entry in the recent Troika Exhibit won a "best of show" award for innovative design. The show at the Cue Gallery will be the first opportunity for the local crafts community to view the full range of Hines's designs following the Troika Exhibit.

"We feel honored to offer the Hines show at the Cue," Elmer Buff, owner of the gallery commented. "Gaylord has opened a new design trend in culinary pottery. He prefers to continue working in utilitarian pieces rather than ceramic art."

The Hines show will continue at the Cue Gallery for four weeks. Following the Sunday preview, the Gallery will be open from 10 A.M. to 5:30 P.M. Free parking is provided behind the building.

Along with the copy enclose a 5 x 7 glossy black and white photo of you alongside a sample of your work, such as Hines's Troika Exhibit winner.

You can see the publicity potential from entering and *winning* competitions. Winning the Troika Exhibit affords Gaylord Hines a "why" for the story about his one-man gallery show.

If you haven't won a prize, consider these examples of leads for publicity—

❖ Mary Anne Sheppard will exhibit her flowercrafts at the ——— Department Store from 3 to 4:30 P.M. daily for two weeks beginning ———. Ms. Sheppard teaches the crafting of flowers from paper and other materials as part of the Cleveland High School adult education program."

❖ Elizabeth Hanratty will demonstrate how to make wire jewelry without soldering at the November meeting of the Island Women's Association at the South Beach Club. In addition to showing members how they may craft their own earrings and other small jewelry pieces, Ms. Hanratty will display the full range of her craftwork.

❖ Peter Petit, ceramicist at the Four Corners Craft Cottage, will participate in the opening of the Hillside Hospital Auxiliary's Holiday Gift Bazaar, Friday, at 2:30 in the foyer of the hospital.

Mr. Petit will exhibit his new collection of flying waterfowl captured in brilliant color.

Select from an array of leads to offer an editor a reason for using your publicity. Tying in with an organization, particularly a charity or benevolent group, opens an opportunity for the women's page editor to use your material in a noncommercial setting. Even if your release material is not used *in toto*, you may present an arts or entertainment editor with material he can blend into a weekly or daily column. Play the percentages. Not all of your releases will be picked up. But if you continue to send catchy releases, many *will* be printed.

Prepare your release professionally. Concentrate on putting down the facts clearly and accurately. Spell names correctly, and double check any dates and times reported. Of course, you will type your release neatly and accurately, double-spaced on plain white bond paper. Send your material to a newspaper or other publication at least two weeks ahead of the event's date.

In the upper left-hand corner of the first page, type your full name, address, and telephone number where you may be reached in the daytime. If you are limiting the time, state the earliest date the release may be used with words like "Release for evening papers of July 5." Ordinarily, you need not specify a release date for routine publicity. If your release extends beyond one page, number the pages and include your name and an identifying line at the upper left corner of succeeding pages. At the bottom of the first page and all other pages except the last, type "MORE" in the center. At the end of the story type "END."

Photographs should be eye-catching, lively, timely, and of professional quality. Try to capture a bit of action in the photo—you at work in your studio, for example. Feature a prize-winning craft entry to add a news break to a release. Ordinarily, a newspaper will not send a photographer to cover an opening or gallery show. You might be photographed as part of a large exhibit or craft fair by a newspaper photographer, but seldom for an upcoming event. Occasionally, if a craftsman furnishes the program for a large or socially important group, a reporter and photographer may cover the event. But don't count on such coverage.

Don't attempt to submit Polaroid or snapshot photos. Prints

should be black and white only with good contrast. Remember, the better the photo, the better your chances of its being published and the better it will reproduce on newsprint. Along with the photo, type (double space) a caption to identify any people (including yourself). Include other important information, such as the prize won by a craft piece exhibited and the organization. But keep captions brief. Tape the typed caption to the back of the photo and fold it over the front. Include your name, address, and telephone number in the upper left corner of each caption.

Where do you send your release? The more places you send your publicity, the more opportunities for exposure you develop. Try these—

❖ Daily newspapers obviously qualify as first choice. If more than one daily newspaper circulates in your community, send the same release to all—and at the same time.

❖ Consider also the weekly shoppers. These weeklies circulate only to small communities within a city or within a specific suburb. If your release is for a gallery opening or show, send it to all shoppers in the area. If the release is for an appearance at a group meeting, send the release to the paper that circulates in that community.

❖ Cover the weekly handouts at hotels and restaurants with a calendar of events, such as *Chicago Guide*. Gallery and craft shows are usually reported in these handouts for out-of-town visitors.

❖ If you or some member of your family works at a big plant or business that publishes a weekly or biweekly newspaper, send a release and photo to that editor and personalize it by noting the relationship to the plant worker.

❖ If your city has a monthly magazine, send a copy of your release there well in advance of publication, as magazine deadlines are weeks ahead of newspapers.

Feature stories require a different approach. Instead of a shotgun scatter to varied media, use the rifle approach aimed at a specific publication. Note the ideas in Chapter 9 about co-operating with a writer or photographer. Features need not be timely in the sense that the story hangs on a specific date. Features depend more on uniqueness, human interest, and do-it-yourself appeal.

Examine the Sunday magazine sections of newspapers and any

magazines published in your area for feature stories about artists or craftsmen. Features rely heavily on photos for their appeal and tell much of their story in short, catchy captions. Take the Jeff Robson story, for example. There the human interest of a craftsman sharing his expertise and time with underprivileged children appealed to the editors. Look for something different to hook an editor. Effective pegs for a feature include such bits as:

❖ A husband and wife team who work together in designing and marketing ceramic macramé beads as a "togetherness" hobby. Too few husbands and wives enjoy the same interests—so, a feature hook.

❖ Wool used in Paula Simmonds' weaving comes from her own sheep, and she selects them for their natural color. A different approach to a common craft plus the warm appeal of animal photos.

❖ Pictures that appear to flicker through the translucent sides of a cube candle result from a unique candle-crafting method. The appeal of a feature story—the different technique and the unusual results.

❖ Classes that attract students in wax modeling for cast jewelry from all over the United States afford a "home-town craftsman attracts national acclaim" lead.

To interest a feature editor, submit a short query, limited to one page preferably. Enclose several photographs of your work and your shop. In the query cover these topics: What you do and why your craft is unique. Suggest a hook lead similar to those noted above. Outline photo possibilities in addition to the shots enclosed. Offer to send the complete article in 1,000, 1,500, or 2,000 words according to the length of feature you've noted in your reading. Although a feature writer for the publication may write the story under his byline, your writing and photographs will make the job easier.

Professional writers learn to make the most of their material, slicing different segments and slanting them for use in more than one publication. You can multiply the opportunities for exposure by borrowing some of their tricks. For example, one feature article may characterize the students who assemble in your studio for classes—retirees looking for a time-absorbing interest, students from a high school, other professionals honing special skills, women and men with a common interest in your craft, or a lawyer, doctor, or other professional relaxing by learning a new skill. A second article could emphasize the designs of your own craft, the prizes they have won in competitions, and feature superb examples in photographs. A third cut might emphasize new tools or techniques you have developed. Moving to a new location or offering a class at a local school or the YWCA offers another possibility for publicity. All of these approaches would be spaced out over a year or more, preferably in different publications.

Aim one feature at the Sunday magazine section—one of the best read sections of a daily metropolitan newspaper. Another, shorter feature built around a personality approach could appear in the women's section of bulky Wednesday or Thursday editions. A local magazine published by an organization, such as the Junior League, affords high-quality circulation among potential craft buyers. A company newspaper features the off-hour pursuits of workers. If yours is a part-time activity, boost your craft among fellow workers through the plant newspaper. Weekly newspapers, either the shopper or suburban types, offer a broad field for features on local residents. When you develop your eye for promotion, intriguing opportunities will begin popping up all around you.

Make the most of one-time events such as the appearance of a book you wrote alone or with others. Local book authors rate special attention in newspapers and on radio and television. If a local store features your kits of craft materials, highlight your demonstrations with a publicity release, possibly a feature article.

National Publicity

Appearances in nationally circulated magazines can build your image outside the local community. Books and articles in general or special-interest magazines are easier to arrange than most craftsmen realize. (Publishing for profit is detailed in Chapter 9.) While getting paid for publicizing yourself doubles the payoff, don't neglect writing as a source of national visibility even when a publication pays nothing or offers only a token fee.

Radio and Television Publicity

Television stations must generate at least a minimum of local programming as a condition for retaining their license. Nearly all radio stations originate most of their programs locally except for national news. As a result, radio and television program directors actively seek personalities and programs of interest to the community. You can bend these needs to your interests in promoting yourself and your crafts. Television appearances, particularly, offer wide exposure and afford visual action not available on radio or in print media. You can gain access to radio and television shows by following these general guidelines:

Systematically search out the range of opportunities among your local radio and TV stations. Identify the radio "talk" shows, particularly those where listeners phone in questions for the guest. Talk shows may not be broadcast during prime time, but they reach a surprising number of people even when aired late at night. Search TV program listings for those shows where guests are interviewed by a show's host. Look also for shows aired by a local personality in a series format. These shows develop faithful viewing audiences and afford great exposure for guests.

Looking at the program listing isn't enough. Watch or listen to each of the potential shows and study the format—types of guests, amount of time allotted to each guest, props allowed or desired, such as books, finished products, and the like, and, of course, the total time a guest is permitted on the air. Assemble the list of the shows on individual file cards with notations on their receptivity to your craft demonstration appearance.

Develop a pecking order among the identified opportunities. You would prefer to be on the most popular television station first. A station associated with a university, a nonprofit group, or an outlet of the Public Broadcast System may deliver fewer but higher quality viewers, so numbers are not all important.

Begin at the top of your pecking order and work through your list by telephoning the program host or director. Briefly describe the reasons you believe your appearance will interest the viewers of his or her program—not why you want to appear. Consider the program director's interest foremost. If you have a new book, use that as an opening wedge. If you've recently won a competition, open with that. If you can offer a craft idea that viewers can try for themselves at home, you're more likely to get a hearing than if you just plan to appear and talk about a few of your designs. Look for a way you can get the viewers involved—by showing them on the air how to form a simple flower wire jewelry, stitchery, macramé belt, or any other specific project in your specialty. If you're shooting for a half-hour workshop-type program, describe a plan to complete step by step one or more craft projects. If you are scheduled to appear at a charity bazaar selling crafts, offer to appear to publicize that event. Program directors prefer to plug some nonprofit or charity affair rather than an individual. Your aim in the first contact is to get an appointment in person. A "yes" at this stage means the battle is half won.

When you visit the studio, take a variety of your crafts along. If you plan to demonstrate a craft project on the air, assemble it in various stages. Then, quickly run through the steps—how you started, the materials needed, the project at some critical stage, the project ready to assemble, and finally the completed item. You've seen how a cooking teacher conducts a class on TV. She doesn't ask the viewer to wait while a cake bakes for forty minutes. The cook already has the finished product cooked when she shows how to put the parts together. You can follow the same scheme. Show the start. Pick up a partially completed piece and work on it through one or more difficult steps. Talk some more. Pick up the piece at a more complete stage and work with it. Finally, show the complete project. By having a project in pieces, you conserve air time—a critical commodity.

In exchange for your appearance, the host will usually plug your book by showing its cover full screen. If you operate a teaching facility, bring a neatly lettered cue card with your name, address, and phone number. Keep lettering within the 3 to 2 proportions of the TV screen. The camera will zoom in on it at some time during the program. This is the exposure you're looking for.

A few hints may help you with your TV appearance. Dress colorfully. Don't wear a white shirt or blouse; a light blue transmits better. If you work in a bright smock, wear it to the studio. The more action you can work into the show, the better. Just sitting and talking with a host fails to take full advantage of TV's potential. If your crafts include colorful examples, bring them along. Arrange a variety of projects on a table with a neutral backdrop to eliminate distractions. The camera will pan over your crafts, or you may point to several as examples of different techniques. Be sure to include small items as well as big ones. Wherever possible, show a utilitarian item in use—weed pots with a dry arrangement in place, for example. Take as many of your tools as you can carry with you to demonstrate how they are used. Of course, you won't carry an electric kiln into the studio. But if you can manage it, try shaping a clay project for the camera. If you carve wood, take a partially completed project and chip away whenever possible. On TV, action remains the key to building viewer interest. Your craft and your flair for showmanship will determine the effectiveness of your time on the air.

Chit-chatting with a radio talk-show host poses different problems. Without video, you must describe your craft in words. The host will help if your craft can be demonstrated to him while you are on the air. Be prepared with cost figures, sources of materials or kits (preferably your own), and answer phone-in questions quickly and honestly. Appearing on a talk show can be a fun experience, so plan to make the most of it.

When you appear on one TV channel, you will probably not be asked to appear on a competing channel soon. However, there is little competition for exposure between television and radio. Further, an appearance on an educational TV channel will probably not block your appearance on a commercial channel or vice versa. Over a year's time, methodically approach all of the TV channels in your area and as many radio shows as you can find time for. Teaching experience will give you confidence and add clarity and organization to your appearance.

Lectures and Talks

Two classes of crafts lend themselves to promotion through lectures and talks to groups of potential buyers. First are those simple, easy-to-learn crafts using paper, driftwood, plastic dipping goo, macramé, mosaic, stitchery, collage, and stick-together jewelry. These crafts permit onstage demonstrations that lead to the sale of kits or materials, as detailed in Chapter 4.

Second are those crafts requiring artistic and technical skills learned over years of experience. Glass blowing, ceramics, metal-crafted jewelry, lapidary, weaving, leatherwork, and silversmithing require long apprenticeships. You can talk about techniques and show examples of different materials and designs, but such major crafts seldom lend themselves to demonstrations. You can, however, develop a talk about your craft and sell finished products at a meeting or simply invite those interested to visit your studio.

Reaching a wide audience on the talk and lecture circuit requires more of your time than a single appearance on television. However, you can distribute mail-back cards, handbills, or a sign-up list to promote your crafts or to capture the names and addresses of your audiences. Sign-up lists or mail-back cards build a mailing list for announcing shows, special sales at your gallery or shop, or the beginning of new classes.

Joining Organizations and Groups

While your natural inclinations may be to remain aloof and apart from your fellow craftsmen, you should recognize the dollar value of a public image and reputation among your peers. One aid in these efforts is to join co-operative groups or associations working to improve the image and status of all craftsmen. In addition to the usual exchange of views and ideas, co-ops sponsor shows, offer frequent opportunities for publicity through actions contributing to community betterment, and support co-op galleries on a continuing or one-time basis.

Numerous crafts fairs began as a result of co-operative action among the craftsmen in a community. If an organization operates a gallery, you would be permitted to show your work as a member on some rotational basis or at shows featuring specific craft media. Gaining entry into the most prestigious groups can be as competitive as gaining access into a juried craft fair. The quality of your craftwork becomes your gate pass.

As a producing professional craftsman, you will be familiar with craft co-ops and other groups currently functioning through the lively grapevine that functions in every community. If you have not participated in the past, examine objectively the potential benefits to you of belonging—visibility for your work and the opportunity to help yourself and others to market your crafts more successfully.

Advertising

One big difference separates publicity or promotion from advertising—money. Since you pay for advertising, plan to make every penny count. Advertising offers far too much to be covered in part of one chapter, but you can learn from successful practitioners in the craft field.

Direct Mail—Selling your crafts, materials, or know-how nationally by mail is detailed in Chapter 7. But you can use direct-mail advertising to sell your crafts and materials locally or to find students for your classes. You might choose to advertise your crafts to earn the selling commission yourself instead of passing along that part of the retail price to a gallery or consignment shop (see Chapter 3).

One potter uses direct mail to sell her culinary pots, imaginative bird feeders, planters, and ceramic owls, birds, and exquisitely crafted small animals. Over a three-month period she crafts a variety of goods from bird feeders at $20 and up to casseroles with styled lids at $75 to $125 to lamp stands at $200 and up. The tiny bird and animal figures retail for $7.50 to $25. She schedules four open houses a year in her home studio and announces dates by direct mail. She mails a single-page flyer to previous buyers, visitors to her studio, and those who sign the attendance list at lectures. She keeps her studio open only from one to five each of three afternoons for the sale.

The mailing piece is simply an 8½ x 14-inch piece of colored stock on which she has drawn a variety of figures in line illustrating her craft products. Essential information—the dates, time, her name and address, and a simple map with directions for finding her out-of-the-way studio—complete the flyer. She draws the figures and hand letters the other information on a plain white sheet in black ink. On the back side, she types her return address in the upper left corner of what will become the address and mailing panel. In the upper right-hand panel she types the required postal information for bulk third-class mailing—post office and permit number. Flyers are printed on colored stock by one of the quickie printers in her area (discussed later in this chapter). Your post office can explain exactly how to prepare the required bulk third-class imprint and how to qualify for bulk third-class mailing. As long as she sends out 200 or more at one time, the postage costs a minimum of 6.1 cents each at press time.

She types addresses on quadruple mailing-label stock available at stationery stores. After folding the printed pieces twice, flyers measure 3½ x 8½. She sticks on one set of the typed address labels. Then she is ready to sort and bundle the flyers in accordance with postal service rules.

Bundles must contain a minimum of ten flyers, and they must be sorted by zip code. The first sort is for all five identical digits. No label is required for this bundle. The next sort is for all flyers going to the same city. This bundle is labeled "Mixed City." The next classification includes more than one city but a zip code with the first three identical digits. This bundle is labeled "SCF" for Sectional Center Facility. The next broader classification is for "State on Face." The Post Office will supply labels, or you can hand letter your own.

Each mailing requires completion of a pink form (available from the Post Office) with your permit number filled in along with the number of pieces, number of pieces per pound, and the total cost. Small flyers are paid for at the minimum per-piece price.

Bulk third-class mail pays off only when you mail many pieces. You can mail individual third-class pieces weighing less than two ounces for about half the cost of first class mail. If the flyer weighs less than one ounce, first-class rates apply. You can decide whether to use bulk third class by figuring alternative costs. If you mail four times a year, the fixed cost for the permit amounts to $7.50. With the difference between bulk third class and individual third class or first class equal to 3.9 cents (10—6.1 cents), you would need to mail 192 pieces to break even, but 200 is the minimum ($7.50 divided by 3.9 equals 192). If you amortize the original one-time imprint fee of $30 over the first year, the break-even quantity increases to 385 pieces for each of four mailings in one year ($15 divided by 3.9 equals 385).

The potter sends an average of 600 flyers to her mailing list at a cost of $36.60 for postage and $25.20 for printing—an average of just over 10 cents direct cost per potential customer contacted. From a quarter to a third of those receiving flyers show up at each sale. If a customer fails to come after receiving four announcements, her name is dropped from the list. Previous buyers often bring guests whose names are added to the list to replace dropouts. People come to buy or they don't come, so the potter closes an excellent ratio of sales per customer. Her system permits her to minimize selling time by concentrating sales activities during three days each quarter—plus the time spent preparing the mailing.

Handbills and Flyers—Direct action through designing and printing your own handbills draws attention and traffic to your shop or reminds visitors to crafts fairs to contact you later. Circulating handbills to shoppers near the Craft Mall (see Chapter 6) drew attention to the new shop. Individual craftsmen involved in the Mall take turns passing out the handbills to passersby. In a waterfront area or public market, handbills distributed by a student hired for the job can direct traffic to your shop. If you and other craftsmen are displaying your crafts in a shopping mall during a holiday season, flyers left at cashiers' counters or distributed to shoppers in parts of the mall away from the craft show will draw interested customers to the area. Handing a printed flyer to an obviously interested visitor at your fair booth may generate a special order or a visit to your studio later. Or distributing handbills in craft stores or related businesses will promote a craft fair if your group is sponsoring a new event.

Handbills and flyers need not be expensive. The appearance of "instant printers" has reduced the cost to $3.95 for one hundred 8½ x 11-inch copies printed on one side of white or colored stock. A thousand copies printed one side costs $14.95 plus tax with a choice of colors available at no extra cost. Prices may vary from city to city. Prepare your copy for an instant printing with black ink on a white stock. Draw on your artistic abilities to sketch or lay out intriguing art for the handbill. Emphasize the name of your shop, fair, or product, and where to find you. Like the news release, include the who, what, where, when, and why of the event or product you're promoting. Once you have the copy inked on white paper, locate an instant printer in the classified section of a telephone directory. Instant printers identify themselves with phrases such as "printing while you wait," "copies in minutes," and the like.

Yellow Pages Advertising—Classified sections of your telephone directory offer another good ad medium. Shops, stores, and galleries can insert a small ad under such classification titles as "Art Galleries," "Arts and Crafts Instruction," "Arts and Crafts Supplies," "Jewelry Designers"—nearly every craft category. Prices vary according to the size of the city, but Yellow Page ads are contracted for a year at a time and paid for by monthly billing to your business phone. Telephone directory classified advertising draws buyers if you repair jewelry, sell craft supplies, or manufacture craft-related products. A bold-face listing with a single line to denote your specialty draws inquiries at a surprising rate. Check with the telephone company for closing dates—usually about four months before the directory appears. You will need a business phone to rate a listing in the Yellow Pages. One disadvantage—you can change the listing only once a year.

Periodical Advertising—Magazines named after cities, such as New York, Atlanta, San Francisco, and others, open yet another avenue for advertising. Galleries, craft shops, instruction studios, and designers find the monthly magazine that circulates locally to be a good source of leads for gallery traffic. Small display ads developed with a distinctive flair and repeated in each issue have built a brisk trade for craftsmen selling quality jewelry, ceramics, glass figures, forged or welded figures, and other crafts selling in the $50-and-up bracket. If your crafts qualify and your studio can be reached easily from most parts of the community, try a small display ad (2- or 3-column inches). Continuity and repetition are important. You're better off running a 1-inch ad ten times than a 10-inch ad once, even though the ten 1-inchers will cost more, due to the discount as space increases. For rates and closing dates, contact the advertising office of the magazine as listed on the masthead. In addition to space rates, you should receive circulation information and a profile of readers.

When developing display ads, consider each one as a small billboard. While long-copy ads pull mail orders, you should aim for quick impact with small display ads. Include a benefit or a big promise in the headline along with your name if you can work it in. A reader must see your ad before he or she can react to your message. One gallery owner uses a hand-printed ad with sharp black-and-white drawings of crafts to attract attention. An eye-catching logo or symbol can build an identification from ad to ad for attracting attention. Or try tilting your printed message out of alignment with the others on the page to attract reader attention. Writing effective ad copy calls for special training and experience. You might try bartering some of your crafts with an advertising copy writer if you plan to spend more than $50 per month on advertising space.

Classified ads in local magazines offer still another medium for craftsmen. See Chapter 7 for details on how to write and place effective classifieds.

Chapter 3

PRICING TO SELL AND
TO EARN A PROFIT

Pricing can make or break your craft business. You can attract buyers, win awards for design innovation, move all kinds of goods, but if your prices are unrealistic, you'll soon fade out of business. If you price your crafts too high, they won't sell in sufficient volume to keep you busy. If you price your crafts too low, you'll wind up working for pennies after paying for materials and overhead. If you are a serious craftsman, pricing strategy is worth studying in depth. Until you resolve any hang-ups regarding pricing and purity of craftwork and fully understand all that goes into pricing your crafts, you will not operate successfully in the craft marketplace. It's as simple as that!

The price you set for your crafts immediately places your valuation on them in crass dollar terms. An exceptionally high price visibly states the value you place on your works. Let's consider an example—

The market value, as distinguished from the intrinsic, inherent, or design value, is the price at which a reasonable volume of your crafts sell in the market. You may value a sterling silver metalcrafted ring at $200. And you may be right! If the ring sells at $200, your valuation of it is confirmed. However, if the ring fails to sell within some reasonable period when offered to a range of potential buyers, the price you have placed on the ring is "out of line." So, what is the "line?" Competition sets a soft line of price comparison—a soft line because handcrafted pieces fit no set pattern. When each piece offers distinctive originality, comparison becomes difficult. Value, like beauty, takes form in the eye of the beholder. Therefore, price depends on a number of important factors, and you should consider them all when offering your crafts for sale:

Environment—Prices of goods tend to reflect their surroundings. Handcrafted originals on display in an exclusive gift shop or department of a fashionable store gain value from other gifts around them. People who shop in such places are usually moneyed people; they expect to pay high prices for exceptional designs and craftsmanship. When your crafts qualify for display in such outlets, you can expect to price each piece high enough to call attention to their exclusive design and quality. Whether a high price for exceptional craftsmanship will return the most spendable cash for your efforts is another trade-off to be determined. Crafts displayed in a gallery that attracts wealthy patrons also gain value in the eyes of the patrons. People with money shop in galleries and stores which build a clientele on good taste and shrewd marketing strategy. To qualify for a spot in such a market, your crafts must exhibit exceptional design originality and craftsmanship.

Materials—Gold jewelry sells for more than sterling because everybody knows that gold costs more than silver. Gold derives a pricing advantage because certain patrons wish to display a more valuable piece, and gold obviously connotes high price. Don't be misled into thinking, however, that poor craftsmanship in gold will inevitably draw more sales than superior craftsmanship in silver. For the differential between gold and silver to hold, craftsmanship and design must be comparable. If they are, the gold piece should be priced significantly higher than the sterling piece. In fact, gold pieces will usually be priced higher than the cost differential of the metals, thereby offering the opportunity to gain a higher return for the same time and effort. Jewelry craftsmen working in gold tend to exhibit higher confidence in their abilities. Designs are frequently crafted more expertly in gold than in silver or one of the lower cost metals. Similar pricing variations due mainly to the inherent differential value of materials will be less obvious in candle crafts, macramé, and other media. Value differences of materials affect final pricing only when the differentials are well known and obvious to both purchaser and observer.

Craftsmanship and Design—Exceptional craftsmanship will be prized by purchasers knowledgeable in the art and will be paid for accordingly. Originality in design and consummate skill in execution will be appreciated by the buyer who selects crafts for display and sale in those outlets catering to buyers with money. When selling crafts to the relatively naive buyer in an informal market, such as one of the arts and crafts fairs, exceptional craftsmanship becomes less of a factor. Eye-catching design appeals to the casual buyer more than craftsmanship. Generally, craftsmanship means less when lower priced goods satisfy an impulse market typical of the carnival atmosphere at crafts fairs.

Reputation—Big-name craftsmen sell their work at higher prices than unknowns. The crafts produced by show winners, by craftsmen with an eye and an ear for publicity, and by those with a flair for promotion attract buyers, and prices paid are high for signed pieces. Therefore, reputation and name affect the prices you can expect from your crafts. Product design and craftsmanship continue to be important, but crafts by name producers sell quicker and at higher prices than comparable crafts by unknowns. If you are interested in greater earnings per hour, don't underestimate the pricing power of promotion.

Pricing Elements

When you consider pricing, look at the basic elements and how they may be allocated under differing marketing programs. The divisions noted in Fig. 1 reflect pricing strategy typical of crafts such as

Fig. 1: Pricing Formulas

| | | Per Cent | |
Wholesale-Retail		Of Retail	Of Wholesale
Materials and Labor	$ 8.00	20	40
Overhead	7.00	17.5	35
Selling Expense	3.00	7.5	15
Profit	2.00	5	10
Wholesale Price	$20.00		100
Retail Markup	20.00	50	100
Total Retail Price	$40.00	100%	200%

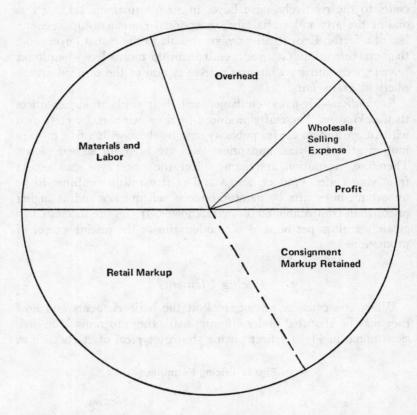

Fig. 2: Division of Retail Price

Overhead

Wholesale
Selling
Expense

Profit

Materials and
Labor

Consignment
Markup Retained

Retail Markup

Division of the retail price pie. Retailer takes half if crafts were paid
for or one third (average) if crafts were stocked on consignment.
See Fig. 1 for division of wholesale price.

jewelry, pottery, weaving, and others requiring skilled design and relatively expensive materials. Examine each of the major elements and the options:

❖ Retail markup—Beginning with the big lump, a retailer who buys crafts for retail will expect to double the price he pays. Remember, markup is figured as a percentage of the final selling price. Thus, the retail markup is 50 per cent—not 100 per cent. Consignment sellers seldom take more than 40 per cent, with 33⅓ per cent common. However, since the craftsman retains title and invests time and materials in crafts displayed for consignment sale, the owning cost becomes part of his overhead. At a consignment markup of 40 per cent, the additional 10 per cent, or $4 in the example detailed in Fig. 1, is added to overhead.

❖ Materials and labor—These are direct costs, unburdened in the language of accounting. Note the direct costs are only 20 per cent of the retail price. This 5 to 1 relationship is relatively common. If you, as the craftsman, execute the design, you earn the labor portion of the direct costs. If you hire the craftsmanship, the labor portion goes to the person executing the design.

❖ Overhead—This bag of miscellaneous charges is detailed elsewhere in this chapter. The cost of these charges cannot be overlooked in pricing crafts, or they will come out of profit.

❖ Selling expense—Even at the wholesale or consignment level, you experience selling expenses for placing your crafts in retail shops. If you hire an agent, this 7½ per cent becomes the agent's commission. The agent will consider the $3 shown in Fig. 1 as 15 per cent of the wholesale price—equal to the 7½ per cent of retail.

❖ Profit—Illusive in pricing schedules, profit represents your compensation for pulling all the pieces together in a business operation. Note the profit is separate from any compensation you might claim for actual production of crafts. If you should operate your own retail shop (see Chapter 6) or sell direct to craft fair visitors, you earn a part of the difference between the wholesale and retail prices. Don't confuse your earnings as a craftsman with profit from the business enterprise or the earnings from selling at retail.

Unless you consider these elements in your pricing, you will experience problems in attempting to move from minor selling on your own to a larger volume distributed through the mail, a retail shop, or on consignment. But if you consider all of these elements, you can operate flexibly and share earnings according to the marketing functions you perform.

Either of two methods may be used to develop the direct costs for your crafts—costs and competition.

Bottom-up Prices—When you base prices on costs, you figure from the bottom up. That is, you compile the cost of materials, compute an allowance for overhead, and set a price that returns a profit. Prices set to recover all costs, including a return for your time, may not sell in competition with crafts priced by amateurs or craftsmen who do not know their full costs.

Top-down Prices—Prices set by competition are figured "from the top down." That is, you shop the market and appraise price schedules for goods similar to the type you plan to produce. Then, you figure backward for material allowances and time. If you can produce within the price constraints of the market, you can figure your profit with fair precision. Let's look at each of these methods in detail:

Pricing to Wholesale

Materials, labor, overhead, and profit comprise the basic elements of wholesale cost for craft goods—and most other products.

Materials may be insignificant, as in copper wire jewelry, or a major element of cost, as in candle crafting. Materials may be only junk—for elements of welded sculptures. But even junk materials incur costs for the time to select and prepare them for use. Materials' costs can be calculated more closely than other cost factors. The sterling that goes into a ring can be weighed and priced precisely, for example. When pricing a first piece, plan to develop an exact accounting of material costs and enter it on the Job Cost Card.

Labor or compensation for your bench time is the second element in pricing. When looking at pricing from the bottom up, set an hourly rate you would like to earn or that you believe represents a fair return for your design skills and craftsmanship. Figure on paying yourself a production rate just as you would expect to be paid if you worked for an employer. When looking at prices from the top down, your hourly earnings depend on production rate.

Overhead puzzles even experienced accountants at times. Overhead comprises all of those costs or time-consuming activities that you know are there but are difficult to assign to individual pieces. Unless you allow for overhead, your prices will be unrealistic or the earnings you believe are there won't show up as deposits in your bank statement. Overhead has a nasty way of sapping earning power. While overhead comprises many elements, the main items are:

❖ Nonproductive time—When you clean up your shop, drive to pick up materials, talk shop with fellow craftsmen, pay bills, send out invoices, and spend time away from your bench at any of dozens of other chores, production of salable crafts suffers. While all of these activities may be important, the time you spend on overhead activities detracts from the time you could have spent producing work for sale. Thus, nonproductive time rates as a cost in terms of lost sales potential to be spread or allocated over those pieces actually produced for sale. Suppose you spend thirty hours a week at your bench actually producing craft pieces for sale and you spend another ten hours at miscellaneous chores. For rational pricing, you must spread those nonproductive hours over the thirty hours of production time. Suppose, further, that you price your work to yield $6/hour of actual bench time; that's $180/week. When you spread nonproductive overhead time over those same hours, you find yourself earning $4.50/hour ($180 ÷ 30 + 10 hours). You can't avoid spending some nonproductive time on your craft business, but your job is to reduce overhead time to an absolute minimum. Your first step in getting a handle on overhead time is to determine how you are now spending your time. Try keeping a minute-by-minute log of how you spend time for a week! Construct a graph of the hours in a day from 7:00 A.M. to 8:00 P.M.—or some similar period. Mark the hours and quarter hours throughout the day and keep the graph handy. When you stop for a coffee break, note the time you start and the time you finish. Do the same for phone calls, time out for meals, bookkeeping, and every other interruption. At the end of each day total the minutes of productive time and nonproductive, overhead time. The equation is simplicity itself. More productive time and less overhead time equal greater earning power. The results will show up in your checkbook.

Fig. 3: Job Cost Card

JOB COST CARD

Job No. __400__ Design No. __000__

Date __11/22__

Description: __STERLING RING with AGATE__   Wholesale Price: __$20.00__

Craftsman: __W.E.J__   No. of Units: __10__

Item No.	Materials	Quantity	Cost
1	Sterling Silver-Grain	2.5 oz.	$15.00
2	Agate Gemstones	10	5.00
			$20.00

	Labor	Hours	Rate	Cost
1	Wax model Preparation	2	6.00	$12.00
2	Casting	2	6.00	12.00
3	Clean-up & Preparation	4	6.00	24.00
4	Gemstone mounting	2	6.00	12.00
				60.00

TOTAL DIRECT COSTS	$80.00
Production Overhead	70.00
TOTAL PRODUCTION COSTS	$150.00
UNIT COST	$15.00
Selling Expense + Profit	5.00
Wholesale Price	$20.00

❖ Space rent—Rent for a shop, store, or other facility remains fixed whether you produce 10 or 110 pieces each week. Many craftsmen work in a home shop to eliminate space cost. But if you are considering renting outside space later, figure an equivalent cost in your pricing. Otherwise, when you move to a shop, you must raise your prices or suffer a decreased income equivalent to the rent.

❖ Utilities and general supplies—Electricity, gas for melting wax or crafting jewelry, packaging materials, office supplies, business telephone—all of these expenses must be paid for out of the price you charge for your goods.

❖ Sales expenses—Advertising, your selling time over a counter or on the phone, commissions paid to salesmen or clerks, and the cost of samples fall into one general category of sales-related costs. To keep them separate, refer to Fig. 1. Salaries or wages paid to sales-clerks in your own shop should be charged to retail sales. Payments for production of crafts are part of direct costs and should not be confused with selling costs. Sales expenses at the wholesale level are amortized over all sales.

❖ Accounting—Keeping books remains a *must* activity today for tax computations and as an essential tool for good business practice. Most craftsmen consider accounting time as a dead loss, or they ignore all but the essentials. Effective accounting benefits pricing and helps you determine the profitability of your business. Instead of attempting to keep books (see Chapter 12), trade some of your craft products for bookkeeping service from an accountant who knows what he is doing, and consider the cost as part of your overhead.

❖ Miscellaneous—Other costs not directly related to each craft piece might cover interest on money borrowed to finance work in progress, inventory, or accounts receivable, an allowance for uncollectible accounts, cost of goods damaged in shipment and returned for repair or replacement, and other petty cash items too numerous to mention. Any business incurs these incidental costs and they are all part of overhead.

Profit finally remains as additional compensation you earn by managing the business. Profit should not be confused with production compensation. Look at the difference this way. If a businessman hired you to craft pieces for sale, you would be paid an hourly wage or by the piece. The manager would supply the materials, provide you with a place to work, and pay all overhead. He would also sell the crafts you and others produced. For his efforts he would earn a profit. As a combination entrepreneur and craftsman, you are entitled to two compensations—a return for your craft bench time and a profit for pulling all of the elements together and managing them to make money.

To build a pricing schedule, begin by collecting data from the production of a prototype or a sample run of pieces using the Job Cost Card. (Fig. 3) Figure the cost of direct materials used in production —the actual cost of sterling silver, wax and pigmentation for candles, cloth and yarn for stitchery, etc. Figure these costs to the penny if possible because you will be extending them to production quantities.

Record accurately the bench time used to produce the sample quantity or prototype. Exclude nonproductive time as this will be figured in an allowance for overhead. Industries determine the time required for manufacturing each element with time cards and job numbers. You can do the same for your shop by noting the elapsed time spent producing the sample quantity and subtracting any nonproductive time.

Production overhead requires more study and possibly a SWEG (that's a Scientific Wild-Eyed Guess). For starters consult the time analysis you kept for a week. Note the proportion of productive to nonproductive time. If you spent one hour on nonproductive activities for each three hours of bench time, increase the actual hours for the sample to allowed hours by one third. Estimate from collected data the money you spend on rent, utilities, accounting, and all the other overhead items noted earlier.

A simple method of spreading these overhead costs to your production items is by direct costs. Collect all of the overhead costs for one month. Again, consult your time analysis. If it shows you engage in 135 actual hours of productive bench time (without the allowance for nonproductive time added), 135 becomes your base. Divide all overhead costs by 135. The resulting figure represents the hourly overhead to be charged in the pricing formula. This will become clearer when we go through an example later.

Finally, figure a reasonable allowance for selling expenses and profit for your entrepreneurial activities. Profit, as noted earlier, will be an addition to your hourly bench rate. You might decide your profit should be 10 per cent or some other rate applied to the accumulated total of costs. On the basis of retail cost, a 5 per cent profit is a goal to shoot at.

Your price can now be figured as:

Materials (M) + Labor (L) + Overhead (O) + Selling Expense (SE) + Profit (P) = Price

Price will be at wholesale.

As an example of how you can apply this formula, consider pricing a group of ten sterling rings with inexpensive stones. Average materials cost for the ten rings for sterling silver and gemstones = $2 or $20 for all ten (see Job Cost Card). While these rings would be individually designed and styled, materials cost would average out to this figure.

Bench time for all ten rings = 10 hours, broken down by activity, as noted on Job Cost Card.

Overhead, figured as a percentage, amounts to 35 per cent, generally a low figure. However, until you collect more definitive data, estimate overhead at 25 to 50 per cent of direct labor or bench time.

Profit can be set at some reasonable figure—say 10 per cent, and wholesale selling expense at 15 per cent (see Pricing Formulas in Fig. 1).

You now have all the elements you need to price the rings, except the value you place on your own bench time. Say you wish to earn $6/hour for your bench time. On this basis, the price for the ten rings figures out to be—

(M) $20 + (L) 10 × $6 + (O) $80 × 35/40 + (SE) $80 × 15/40 + (P) $80 × 10/40 = Price

$20 + $60 + $70 + $30 + $20 = $200 (ten rings) or $20/ring at wholesale

Note that production overhead, profit, and selling expense are ratioed to direct costs. Using the wholesale percentage figures from Fig. 1 as a guide, overhead (O) equals 35/40 of direct cost because direct costs amount to 40 per cent and overhead is set at 35 per cent of the wholesale price. Thus, overhead will be 35/40, or 87.5 per cent, of the $80 direct costs, or $70 in the example detailed in Fig. 3. Selling expense (SE) and profit (P) reflect similar ratios or percentages of direct costs. The pricing formula in Fig. 1 represents an example only, as the division between direct costs and overhead will vary according to craftsman and craft.

Retail price for these rings would run $40, figured at double your wholesale cost. If you sell the rings yourself through your own retail shop, at one of the arts and crafts fairs, or by mail, you could figure on earning the difference between production cost of $20 and retail price of $40 for your retail selling efforts. If you sold your rings through a consignment shop that took one third of the retail price, your total price would be $26.67 with the additional $6.67 over the wholesale price as compensation for financing the inventory stocked until sold by consignment shops (see Chapter 4) and added record keeping.

Note these points in this pricing schedule:

❖ Retail price will be double your total cost of production—typical for most crafts. Wholesale might be 60 per cent of retail for candles and some crafts where material costs form a large part of the total price. Jewelry is typically marked up 50 per cent of retail price.

❖ Wholesale price accounts for all factors—materials, bench time, overhead, selling expense at wholesale, and profit.

❖ Wholesale price depends largely on the dollars allowed for time and overhead—$130 ($60 + $70) or 65 per cent of the total price for ten rings represents compensation for your time and miscellaneous charges in this example.

❖ Selling costs at the retail level are figured in addition to your costs for production only. Even if you sell your crafts at retail, figure those selling costs separately from production costs as detailed above. Selling retail involves other costs as detailed in Chapter 6. When you price your work at wholesale, you have the option of selling it at that price to others who, in turn, sell it at retail to earn their compensation or to sell it yourself and earn additional compensation. Selling expense at wholesale can be relatively small because crafts are sold in large quantities. An agent's fee for wholesale lots is typically 15 per cent of the wholesale price. Many craftsmen leave marketing to those gallery or shop owners skilled in merchandising.

You may find sterling rings with stones in a variety of designs selling at galleries and shops for around $40. If so, you can figure your prices are in line with competition. But let's examine other possibilities.

Suppose, for example, that producing the ten rings required 20 hours of bench time instead of 10. Following the same pricing formula noted in Fig. 1 the total price would then escalate to—

(M) $20 + (L) 20 × $6 + (O) $140 × 35/40 + (P) $140 × 10/40 + (SE) $140 × 15/40 = Price
$20 + $120 + $122.50 + $35 + $52.50 = $350 or $35 each

With a wholesale price at $35, each ring would need to sell at retail for $70 or thereabouts. If similar rings were selling for $40–$50, your rings would not sell because their retail price would be out of line.

Should you find your pricing out of line, you could be faced with several alternatives—

❖ Increase your production rate to craft the rings in less total time. When figuring the time for an initial sample quantity, you will find that you are likely to be high on the "learning curve." As you produce more of the rings, you will pick up time, and production for a second quantity of ten rings should require less time than for the initial ten rings. Therefore, allow for improved production rate as you work down the learning curve when pricing from an initial sample quantity. Experience will help relate production time for a prototype or initial run to later production time.

❖ Reduce your hourly rate. Instead of $6/hour, you would have to cut your expected hourly rate to $3/hour to compete in the market for rings priced around $40 retail in the second example.

Expected hourly rate and actual production time remain the key elements in the pricing formula. You could reduce overhead time for a small improvement. Another alternative would step up your normal work week to 40 hours of bench time. Any overhead activities or nonproductive time would add hours to your work week but would not detract from productive bench time. Eliminating profit altogether would reduce prices, but you're kidding yourself if you do. The main reason for keeping books and knowing your costs to the penny is to help you make businesslike decisions from facts rather than hunches or emotion.

Production rate, that is, the number of salable pieces turned out in one hour's time, shapes up as the key factor in how much money you make producing crafts. Look at this example:

A precise silversmith might spend 10 hours designing and crafting an original choker necklace with a materials cost of $20. If this craftsman values his time at $10/hour, he would sell the choker for $350 wholesale after allowances for overhead, selling expense, and profit. The retailer would mark up the piece to $700. Even in stores or galleries where moneyed people shop, not too many $700 chokers are sold day in and day out. If similar pieces could sell profitably for $300, demand would likely be more brisk. However, if the craftsman sold his work for $175 to permit a retail sale at $350, he would earn only $5/hour gross for his time, plus allowances for overhead and profit, after paying the $20 for sterling.

If, instead of producing only one choker in 10 hours of bench time, this same craftsman was able to design and fabricate three similar but distinctively different chokers based on one original idea, he could price the chokers at $175 at wholesale with a retail selling price of $350. After subtracting $60 for materials, he retains $150 for 10 hours' bench time plus $52.50 profit. Crafting three pieces in the time normally required for one may appear impossible, but craftsmen who understand the working of the pricing formula produce efficiently to increase their earnings. Further, the three sterling chokers will not be mass production pieces. Each choker will emerge with its own distinctive design variation. But making three pieces at once permits shortcuts not available during one-at-a-time crafting. When you appreciate the value of an hour's bench time, you begin to find ways of accomplishing work in less time. In effect, you learn to work smarter, quicker, and harder.

Pricing to Compete

Pricing "from the top down" uses the same elements in the pricing formula—except you start with the final price and work backwards. The relation between materials, productive time, overhead, selling expense, and profit still apply. Pricing from the top down calls for a precise understanding of the market. Begin by surveying your competition. Find out which crafts are selling, in what quantity, and at what prices. Your market research may examine the retail market or the wholesale market. At a trade show for candle crafts, for example, note the prices of the different types, sizes, and designs of candles offered for resale. Prices will be at the wholesale level. Thus, you need not apply a markup to reach your own selling price.

During your market research look for crafts similar to yours in general design, use of materials, and craftsmanship. When originality of design figures prominently in the price, you will find a considerable spread between pedestrian designs at the low end and highly original, striking designs at the high end. If your crafts match or exceed those being offered at the high end of the design scale, set your prices at the high end of the range, as these are the competitive crafts by other producers. Don't feel you must undercut the market or pricing; remain open-minded and completely realistic during your survey. If you fool yourself into pricing your pieces in the wrong category, you lose. You may need to experience the competitiveness of the market in pricing your crafts before you become an expert.

Suppose that, after your market research, you find sterling rings with stones of the type you plan to produce selling wholesale at $36 each. From your previous study you figure materials at $1.80/ring, so the remaining $34.20 must cover bench time, overhead, and profit. Working with percentages from the top down becomes a little easier than from the top up. Note:

Profit at 10 per cent =	$3.60
Selling expense at 15 per cent =	5.40
Overhead at 35 per cent =	12.60
Materials =	1.80
Labor =	12.60
Total	$36.00

Bench time becomes a critical element. If you produce ten rings in 15 hours, you earn $8.40 [(10 × $12.60) ÷ 15 = $8.40]. But if you spend 25 hours producing ten rings, your bench rate drops to $5.04/hour.

Either from the top down or from the bottom up, pricing schedules emphasize the direct relationship between productivity and earnings. Unless you learn to produce items for sale with reasonable bench times, hourly rates of return for your labor will likely be unattractive.

Producing craftsmen find themselves competing with amateurs in many markets. Pricing formulas may be difficult to apply when your competition is more interested in visibility and recognition than a satisfactory rate of return for their time. Amateurs or hobbyists will frequently price their crafts at some level close to the actual cost of materials purchased in small quantities at retail rates. These craftsmen consider replacement of materials as their prime objective. Frankly, such attitudes and pricing policies create serious problems for producing craftsmen attempting to earn a reasonable return for their work. Head-to-head competition with amateurs or hobbyists will most likely occur in local arts and crafts shows, in benefit bazaars at Christmas time, or in consignment shops operated by nonprofit charity organizations. Buyers exposed to low price levels at such events cannot be expected to understand prices that include costs for all factors of production—including a fair return for the craftsman's bench time. Your best bet is to avoid such head-to-head competition and concentrate on other routes of distribution. Achieving a name and reputation for your work also takes you out of the head-to-head competition with amateurs and hobbyists. Frequently you will find hobbyists who turn out exquisite works yet price their crafts at piddling prices. A talk with these persons about pricing could influence them to set more realistic prices for their work, even if they are not primarily interested in earning cash from their crafts.

Pricing formulas may vary from the one detailed in Figs. 1 and 3, if you distribute your crafts through certain channels. For example, if you rely heavily on selling through consignment shops, you should allow for returns and damage to your work. For example, stitchery or weaving crafts are subject to handling deterioration. A potential customer in a consignment shop offering woven goods, for example, expects to feel the texture. A cape woven of fluffy, soft cashmere or llama wool soon shows signs of wear if enough customers feel and fondle the cape. After three or four months, the cape appears shopworn, and the shop owner returns it to the weaver with "Sorry." The weaver might offer the cape as a "second" or consider the whole project as a loser. Any similar costs must be considered in pricing. The difference between wholesale and consignment sale (66⅔ less 50 per cent of retail price) compensates the craftsman selling on consignment for returns and other costs—*as long as the basics are figured on wholesale price*. The basics are materials, bench time, overhead, wholesale selling expense, and profit. However, if the craftsman figures these factors on a consignment sale price and never sells at wholesale, then the overhead allowance must cover returns, shipping expenses, and losses due to nonsales and damage while on display.

Included separately in the pricing formulas to reach wholesale price is a factor for selling at the *wholesale level*. This selling effort is different from the markup allowed the retail seller. If you sell at the wholesale level (50 per cent off retail price) by mail or through agents, you must include some provision for handling, marketing by mail, or commissions paid to an agent. For example, suppose you sell your crafts to retail shops by mail. Your price is 50 per cent of retail. You may add shipping to your costs when billing a retail shop, but you must include an allowance for marketing your crafts prior to an actual shipment. Marketing efforts might include direct-mail advertising or promotion, attendance at a buyer's show where you pay for display space, travel expenses, long distance telephone tolls, entertainment of buyers, development and production cost of brochures, order forms and other paperwork, and costs associated with distribution—returns, possible damage, bad debts, and inventory financing. All of these costs must be included in the allowance for selling expense when you figure your wholesale pricing schedule. If you fail to allow for these cost factors, your earning rate/hour for bench time must absorb these extra costs.

Records of materials costs, labor spent on each item or group of items, detailed selling expenses, and other bookkeeping become tiresome and a drag on your total costs. Use the Job Cost Card and produce your crafts in reasonable job lots to reduce accounting time. Quickie rule-of-thumb pricing may be easier, but you can fool yourself easily. The Job Cost Card simplifies the task of keeping precise records that keep your prices competitive.

Elasticity of demand is a concept basic to economics relating volume to price and earnings. It answers the question "If I dropped my price, would I sell enough additional pieces to earn more spendable cash?" Generally, crafts are priced too low already to generate additional profits by lowering the price. Instead of lowering prices, you might find total return (bench earnings plus profit) increasing at higher prices. Remember, your aim is to earn a fair return, not necessarily increase sales. Instead of concentrating on volume production entirely, consider the added sales potential or unique design or a combination of design and materials that yields unique pieces to sell. When your craft pieces offer unusual or unique designs, you essentially escape competition because no one sells goods directly comparable to yours. This is one reason that artistic ceramicists graduate to artistic expression from production of pots, casserole dishes, etc. Art forms in ceramics can be completely original and thus escape direct comparisons of pricing for utilitarian usage.

Experiment judiciously, if you must, with price changes to increase volume of sales. Sometimes a "price leader" generates interest or traffic in your crafts. Once people are attracted to your crafts, they will often "buy up"; that is, buy one of your pieces that carries a normal markup. You can notice this tendency when selling direct at arts and crafts shows. Rather than jiggle prices, you can probably increase your profits by working smarter and harder to turn out more pieces exhibiting high craftsmanship for sale at normal markups.

Amateurs give themselves away at pricing. Amateurs will haggle, hem 'n haw, and ask such silly questions of buyers as "Well, what do you think it's worth?" As a result, amateurs and hobbyists deflate price schedules, and buyers, retail or wholesale, take advantage of them.

A buyer of crafts for sale in a tasteful shop that sells a line of high-quality merchandise observes, "Craftsmen walk in with armloads of goods, hawking their crafts like little children begging for candy. Merchandising is a business. I ask a craftsman about his price if his goods interest me. More often than not, this craftsman asks me to set the price by asking something like 'What do you think you can sell it for?' I have a pretty good idea of what I can sell various craft items for in our shop from experience—but that's my business, not his."

Pricing techniques and strategy are important enough to warrant spending considerable time studying and applying the results of your studies. Experienced, producing craftsmen understand the importance of pricing and generally offer these tips:

❖ Wholesale price will generally run from double to 120 per cent more than the direct cost of production—that is, the out-of-pocket cost of materials and your direct labor. The added factor accounts for overhead and profit.

❖ Retail price will be double the wholesale price. By this rule of thumb, retail price is four to five times the direct cost of production. Some craftsmen use the factor of five for pricing from direct costs when selling by mail.

❖ Price variations for your goods in various shops can result in lost markets. A discounting outlet that prices your goods at 15 to 25 per cent under prices maintained in major outlets can lead to cancellations by those outlets you prize most. Therefore, you should maintain some surveillance over prices charged at retail. You cannot legally control prices at retail, but you can discontinue selling to those outlets that discount your goods by one ruse or another.

❖ When in doubt, go up in price rather than down. You'll find it easier to adjust prices downward if initial prices are off target than to raise them later.

❖ Competition will affect your pricing schedules more than cost of production. Therefore, when competition forces prices downward, you must either offer a product sufficiently unique to lift it out of direct competition or learn every shortcut possible to reduce costs and earn a satisfactory return for your bench time plus a profit.

❖ Earnings and profits remain the primary objective of pricing—not sales merely for the sake of sales. How you price your crafts affects your earnings as much as any other single factor in your business.

Chapter 4

SELLING YOUR CRAFTS THROUGH
SPECIALTY CHANNELS

Marketing crafts can be fun for both beginning and professional craftsmen at the summer arts and crafts fairs. Plus—and it is a big plus—fairs offer one of the most lucrative and handy outlets around for your craft products. Fairs offer a *pot pourri* of painting, crafts in nearly every media, artists and craftsmen in action—and blueberry pie with ice cream when patrons tire of stalking sidewalks and aisles crammed with exhibits.

Arts and crafts fairs dot summer weekend activity calendars all over the United States. Artists and craftsmen unite to bring their work to the public in an outdoor arena. Merchants co-operate because customers flock to exhibits by the thousands and spill over into stores. In the Seattle-Puget Sound area, at least one arts and crafts fair is scheduled for every weekend from early June through September. The big daddy of Pacific Northwest fairs is the Bellevue Arts and Crafts Fair. Held each July in Bellevue, Washington, it has become one of the most popular and best attended of all the fairs in the United States. During a recent fair, close to 150,000 attended during the three days. A look at how this fair operates will show you how you can sell your crafts this fun way.

The Bellevue fair runs from Friday through Sunday afternoon with Friday evening the big night. Crowds throng the central Bellevue Square area. Streets are blocked off. Kiosks and booths accommodate craftsmen from all over the Pacific Northwest. Jewelry and pottery vie for honors as the favorite craft—along with hundreds of paintings, sculpture, and films.

Artists and craftsmen in action demonstrate their talents and skills as key features at arts and crafts fairs. A woodcarver chips away at a cedar log with a half-formed whale beginning to emerge from his seemingly aimless chipping. Adults and children watch for hours as chips fly from chisel and ax. A popular jeweler whangs away forging designs on pendants with a ball-peen hammer on an anvil. The ringing sounds and action draw visitors who may buy enameled earrings for 50 cents a pair or sterling silver rings in the $20, $25, and $50 price range. A silhouette artist quickly snips a profile from black paper while her model sits seemingly oblivious to the throngs of passersby. Artists paint comic designs on clean water-smoothed beach rocks near a craftswoman dipping wire frames in plastic to form flowers and leaves while visitors watch intently.

Fairs offer craftsmen opportunities to sell their goods with a minimum sales fee. Sales at the Bellevue Arts and Crafts Fair gross in excess of $120,000 during the three-day event. Between eighty and one hundred craftsmen participate along with hundreds of artists and sculptors in three divisions. One jewelry craftsman grossed $1,500 in three days. A batik craftswoman sold $800 worth of scarves and fabrics. Craftsmen pay only a 20 per cent commission on sales during the three days—no commissions on sales of custom goods delivered later.

Exhibitors in the Craft Mall occupy from one to four 4-x 8-foot booths and sell finished crafts. Artists-in-Action work in 6-x 10-foot modular sections to create their craft products on site. They also sell previously crafted products.

Many craftsmen began their selling activities and built a clientele at the Bellevue fair or one of the others in the Puget Sound area. Craftsmen can earn a major share of their annual income from sales during the summer festival season. They produce stock for sale months in advance because of the fair's low-cost marketing potential.

The Pacific Northwest Arts and Crafts Association (PANACA) sponsors the Bellevue fair. To assure quality arts and crafts, the shows are juried; that is, each craftsman submits representative work for screening. The jury selects exhibitors according to a number of criteria:

First, the jury insists on a variety of craft media. Competition among entrants in certain media rages more intensely than in others.

Pottery, extremely popular in the Pacific Northwest, draws more competition than woodcarving, for example. Handcrafted jewelry, particularly silversmithing, is another popular and extremely competitive media.

Second, craftwork must meet high design and fabrication standards. Representative designs and techniques within each of the craft media add further variety in screening.

Third, since expenses for staging the fair are paid from commissions on sales, popular crafts and arts known to appeal to visitors will be included to assure sales. Although sometimes denied, most experienced craftsmen are well aware of this criterion.

Screening occurs in April for the Bellevue fair the following July. Circulars announcing dates for submission of crafts for screening publicize the dates among artists and craftsmen. Usually, entries are screened on a Sunday. At last count only about one in four of the craft entrants made it into the fair. A pecking order develops among the fairs in the region with the most popular fairs drawing the most competition—and the best opportunities for sales. Beginners find entry easier at the smaller, less well-known fairs. With the summer arts and crafts fairs growing and new ones opening every summer, you will find these fairs a great chance to break into selling. Along with sales potential, most producing craftsmen look forward to the fairs as an opportunity to see what other craftsmen are designing and to test the market appeal of their new ideas.

Fairs award prizes to winners of various categories to provide further income opportunities. At the Bellevue fair during a recent summer, artists competed for $2,700 in prizes in three divisions—professional, nonprofessional, and junior. Out-of-town jurors select prize winners to avoid local prejudice. In the crafts fields, $2,000 in prizes were awarded to works in different media. Awards were in open jury competition, Craft Mall, and Artists-in-Action. A junior division in crafts encourages student work.

Craftsmen must bring all of their own gear, such as a table, showcase, or bench, although electrical service can usually be arranged. Display space for artists' work is provided along sidewalks and in a center pavilion. An Artist-in-Action may set up an easel and other facilities for painting portraits. A silk-screen printmaker may set up his full operation within a booth space and demonstrate his technique to passersby.

On the other side of the nation, the Northeast Craft Fair, begun in Vermont, has moved to the Dutchess County Fairgrounds at Rhinebeck, New York. It holds forth in June each year. The Northeast Craft Fair (NECF) limits participation to craftsmen from the eleven states of Maine, Connecticut, Delaware, Maryland, Massachusetts, New Hampshire, New Jersey, New York, Pennsylvania, Rhode Island, and Vermont, plus the District of Columbia.

The NECF differs in a number of significant ways from the usual craft fair as exemplified by the Bellevue Arts and Crafts Fair—

❖ At Rhinebeck visitors pay an admission fee, recently one dollar. The enclosed fairgrounds permit the area to be closed off for crowd control. Approximately 50,000 visitors passed admission gates at a recent fair.

❖ The NECF extends a full week, but the first two days are limited to wholesale buyers. At a recent fair 1,200 buyers from gift and craft shops, department stores, and galleries bought or contracted for $1.1 million of crafts at the wholesale price level. Some craftsmen delivered goods directly to wholesale buyers, but most took orders for later delivery. The public bought an estimated $120,000 at retail prices during the remainder of the week. The $120,000 represented a doubling of retail sales from the previous year, first for the NECF at Rhinebeck. Some craftsmen reportedly sell half to two thirds of their annual production either at the fair or on orders taken at the fair.

❖ No percentage of gross sales is deducted from craftsmen's sales either during wholesale or retail sales days. Financing of the fair is mainly through admissions and booth rental fees. Three types of craftsmen's booths are available, and they are all about 10 x 10 feet in area. Booths inside fairground exhibition buildings rent for $75 for the week. Similar booths under cover of large commercial tents rent for $60. Outside, uncovered booth spaces rent for $45. All sales and orders written are handled individually by the individual craftsmen. NECF requires that the craftsman who produced the work displayed attend the booth for the duration of the fair.

Objectives of the fair reflect the philosophy of the group of craftsmen who originated it in Vermont and managed it with volunteers during its first eight years. A paid director now plans and manages the NECF at Rhinebeck. Fair concepts are embodied in its stated objectives:

❖ To afford professional craftsmen of the Northeast region a place to exhibit and sell handmade objects.

❖ To offer craft shop owners and gallery directors an opportunity to purchase contemporary crafts in one central location.

❖ To offer the general public an opportunity to purchase objects from a wide selection of handmade crafts, and to give all visitors to the fair a better understanding of the contemporary craft movement in the hope that this will increase their appreciation of handmade objects in general.

❖ To bring craftsmen of the eleven northeastern states and the District of Columbia together for an exchange of ideas and a sharing of interests.

Gaining entry to the NECF requires first that a craftsman belong to the American Crafts Council and live in the Northeast region. Potential exhibitors meeting the first two requirements then submit five color slides of the work they intend to exhibit. The slides are reviewed by a nine-member Selection Committee, which is directed to make their selections according to the following statement of standards: "Whether produced in quantity or as an individual piece, the ideal work reflects excellence. The work should be well-conceived and expertly executed without technical faults. The work should show imagination and the mark of individuality." The usual deadline for submission of applications is the January before the June fair. In a recent year over 900 craftsmen applied and less than 500 were accepted for showing in the fair—so competition is keen.

Craftsmen in Action provide much of the entertainment and action for NECF visitors as they do at other fairs. One year Josh Simpson, glass craftsman, towed his glass furnace from his studio in Connecticut. He demonstrated his techniques and provided molten glass for blowing to other glass craftsmen as well. Tie-dying and many other craft skills were also demonstrated throughout the fair.

Since summer arts and crafts fairs offer such great opportunities to sell your crafts, develop your plan to participate.

First, survey the fairs within a reasonable distance from your shop. You probably are already familiar with local shows, if any. But look beyond your community fairs. Craftsmen come from as far as four hundred to five hundred miles to participate in the Bellevue fair and from all over the Northeast to Rhinebeck. Write for entrance information, cost, prizes awarded, and instructions for submitting your crafts for screening. Henry Niles publishes a "National Calendar of Indoor-Outdoor Art Fairs," and "National Calendar of Open Art Exhibitions" ($10 a year each) updated quarterly that lists locations, dates, fees, and addresses. For the latest calendar, write to Henry Niles, 5423 New Haven Avenue, Fort Wayne, Indiana 46803.

Second, if you decide to participate, your first objective is to get in. Unless a fair is juried, you'll find a mixture of simple handicrafts, quickie and quaint pieces, and true crafts. Therefore, if there's a choice, pick the juried show and submit your best work for screening. Include a variety of your craft products and indicate if you plan to work as a "Craftsman in Action" at the fair. Remember, one of the criteria is the appeal of your work to buyers. You are interested in selling and so are fair sponsors. Your entries will be screened on the basis of your submitted work, but publicity and a résumé of past shows or gallery exhibitions sometimes help to sway jury decisions.

Third, when selected to participate, plan your booth to offer the best visibility for bench action. Dramatize your booth, as action and staging attract visitors. The more visitors you attract, the more crafts you are likely to sell. The jeweler who forges big brass medallions on a ringing anvil pulls buyers in from a wide area. One of the most popular booths at the Bellevue fair is a do-it-yourself pottery booth. Benches around a large square afford buyers the chance to decorate their own coffee mug or flower bowl with glazes. Then, their designs are fired on the mug or bowl while they watch. The portable kiln is fueled from a propane tank. Within minutes the customer's design is fused and allowed to cool. Each buyer can then take away his own unique product for less than $10. The roar of the kiln plus action at the booth never fail to attract a crowd. While near the booth, buyers select from pottery displayed by the operators of the do-it-yourself kiln.

Fourth, display your work to show off your products to their best advantage. Hang batik scarves and fabrics from overhead lines to flow in the breeze. Pottery and ceramics can be arranged according to size. Rather than display small pieces in front, such as weed jars or tea mugs, place them at the back to forestall shoplifting. Big, heavy pieces around the edges are difficult to carry away unnoticed. Display jewelry only behind a glass or plastic case to prevent pilferage. Small, inexpensive items, such as the enameled disks for earrings, can be left out in the open because they will not contain ear screws or ear wires. These are attached according to a buyer's preference. At least two people should attend each booth at all times—one for action and one to "mind the store." When designing your display, remember you will be setting it up, taking it down, and hauling it yourself. While tables and shelves may remain overnight, you will want to remove your valuable goods for safekeeping elsewhere each night.

Fifth, promote your crafts for sale later. Offer to take special orders for custom crafts to suit a buyer's individual interest. Some exhibitors take orders without a deposit. They figure the product will sell even if a custom buyer fails to pick it up. Other craftsmen insist on a small down payment, perhaps only 10 per cent of the agreed price, to commit the buyer and to weed out the casual or impulsive purchaser. If you already have a business card, keep stacks of them available to be picked up. Or create a single sheet or inexpensive folder that describes your product line, maps the route to your out-of-the-mainstream workshop, and includes a short résumé of your experience and training. If you offer custom designs, repairs (jewelry or antiques), classes, or materials, state these facts in your folder. If you have authored a book or a folder of lesson plans, offer them along with your craft products. A shelf of brightly jacketed books draws spectator interest and authenticates your craft expertise. Other craftsmen in your media will buy the book, but not your crafts. Folders can be printed inexpensively with one of the new "instant print" systems. You'll find that young paper collectors will pick up one of everything offered, so don't spend more than two to three cents a copy for promotion folders. If your work is being exhibited at a gallery, hand-letter a showcard to promote your gallery exhibit at the fair. The more traffic your show generates for the gallery, the sooner you will be invited back.

Your personal activity at an arts and crafts fair can help or hinder sales. A booth displaying only a few products and a clerk or the craftsman lolling in a chair drinking coffee with a bored look seldom attracts serious buying interest from passersby. Exhibiting your crafts is not enough, you must *sell* them. Why spend the effort to gain entrance to a fair and then ignore potential customers? Keep busy at the booth, even if you only rearrange pieces. A better image is to keep working on something. You not only generate interest, but you keep producing goods for sale. Be aggressive in selling. You need not hawk your goods like a sideshow spieler, but if a visitor shows the slightest interest, tell her about your products, pull items out of a display case to show. Ask a customer about her interests. Volunteer information about a stone in a colorful pendant or show how a batik scarf can be combined with a special pin—anything to encourage the looker to buy your goods. Learn the subtle techniques of "the close," asking indirectly for an order or sale. You are the salesman. If selling does not come naturally, invest some of your winter evening time in an adult evening course in selling; the training will pay magnificent dividends the next summer.

Just a few more hints—

❖ Be prepared for a variety of weather. If your fair is blessed with bright sunshine and your assigned space is open, protect yourself against sunburn—a wide-brimmed hat, a patio umbrella to shade your work location, or some temporary overhead shade.

❖ Hours tend to be long, so be prepared with Thermos bottles of coffee and possibly a lunch unless you can arrange for shifts.

❖ Ask about shelter in case of rain. Some fairs are scheduled in school buildings or open-sided areas under roof overhangs. If your booth space does not include a roof, carry a plastic tarp and poles to hold it in place. If the grounds are not paved, you may need to cover the area with sawdust, hay, or portable planking if the area turns to mud.

❖ Wear comfortable, casual clothing, possibly bright clothing to play the part of the craftsman.

❖ Consider the arts and crafts fairs as fun outings and reflect the gaiety of the crowd. Visitors frequent arts and crafts fairs to look and to have fun as well as to buy. Picking up their mood encourages sales.

With so many arts and crafts fairs around, how do you decide which ones are worth the effort? If your objective is to sell your crafts and maximize the income potential from your time and effort, look at these variables that could affect your sales success at fairs:

❖ Fair history and longevity—Fairs with established track records for attendance tend to attract "buying crowds." As fairs continue from year to year, their reputation spreads and crowds build. So, the older the fair the better as long as it is active, aggressively promoted, and innovative. Curiously, large crowds tend to be buying crowds, while sparse attendance inhibits sales.

❖ Location—Attending a fair can be an impulse activity for many, so a fair in a handy location, close to major arterials, or near places where people normally congregate will draw more people than a fair stuck out of the way and far from the action.

❖ Sponsorship—Craft association sponsorship elevates a fair to a noncompetitive activity and draws visitors friendly to crafts. Nonprofit associations gain access to promotion possibilities far easier than fairs that charge admission or are obviously profit oriented. Church and charity groups may sponsor a fair with the idea of raising money for good purposes. Unfortunately, once visitors have paid admission, they may feel they have discharged their obligation— and little buying takes place.

The ideal fair is one which screens or juries entries, is promoted and publicized as a cultural event, and consistently draws a buying crowd. A fair's past performance can provide clues. Ask others who have participated previously before deciding which of several alternatives offer the best sales opportunities.

County and regional fairs feature craft exhibits along with livestock, flowers, and farm crops. Like the arts and crafts fairs, they afford visibility for you and your craft products. Some fairs offer only the opportunity to exhibit entries for judging—quilts, for example. But with the burgeoning interest in crafts, more fairs are opening their halls to practicing craftsmen, similar to the craft malls at arts and crafts festivals.

Typically, county fairs hold forth in the fall, sometimes for three days, sometimes for nine or ten days spanning two weekends. Check with the fair director in your county about plans for a craft mall or Craftsmen in Action. County fair directors are recognizing the attractions of craftsmen and are setting aside special sections. If the fair runs for ten days, make sure you can spend the time profitably by having enough stock to support sales over the full period. If possible, arrange your booth or kiosk to permit continued production during slow periods. One quilter in Missouri sold enough custom jobs at her county's fair to keep her busy designing and sewing quilts throughout the rest of the year. If direct selling is not permitted, display your name, address, and telephone number prominently to cue direct inquiries later.

Lectures and Demonstrations

Craftsmen who work in jewelry, flower, or papercraft, and other media which lend themselves to lectures can tap almost unlimited opportunities for demonstrations and sales to women's clubs and study groups. Lucile Edmonds teaches the crafting of paper flowers at a small shop in a suburban district. Rather than sell finished products, she sells the materials separately and in kits.

"There's one thing you have to remember about crafts," Lucile cautions. "If the craft looks simple enough to do yourself, a person would rather make it than buy it. That's true of knitting, stitchery, macramé, beadcraft, flowercraft, and others."

One of Lucile's marketing ploys is to schedule appearances at women's club luncheons or as the program at a club meeting in the afternoon or evening. Drawing on her experience as a teacher, she developed a fast-paced lecture-demonstration on the crafting of a variety of gaily colored flowers. She begins her talk by displaying a number of different creations that never fail to draw admiring "aahs and ohs."

"Now," she says, "I'm going to show you how you can make these flowers too!" As she crafts one of the simpler flowers onstage, she describes each step precisely—sometimes tossing in a comic comment. Once she finishes the basic technique, she moves on to describe a number of variations. She aims to show how easy the technique really is and the variety available from a few deft twists and turns. As a finale, she invites questions, then closes with her "commercial message." In about three minutes she describes her beginner class priced at only one dollar per session. Originally she offered free lessons, but soon found that a nominal charge attracted more participants. Many people equate price with value. "If the lessons are free, too many interested persons figure they are worth just that—nothing," she relates.

Kits are packed with complete, detailed instructions, but her major sales come from women who attend her classes. There, she includes basic materials for a simple flower as part of the class fee. Interested women buy the kits for continued work at home. They return again and again to buy more materials and to learn more advanced techniques. Class lessons after the first cost three dollars each and are limited to ten persons. Although the materials are reasonably priced, they include a 66⅔ per cent markup of retail and the volume pays off handsomely. However, because papercraft tends to be self-limiting in design possibilities and skills, she must continue to attract new customers. Hence, her move to lectures and demonstrations rather than advertising. Here are the basic elements of Lucile's marketing strategy:

Women's clubs and groups abound in cities and suburbs and they are constantly looking for program ideas. With no budget to pay for speakers, a program chairman soon runs dry of interesting ideas. Clubs welcome Lucile as a no-cost guest speaker. Rather than object to the "commercial" at the end, they endorse the idea of introducing club members to new and exciting craft activities. She can pick and choose her opportunities. During the fall and winter season she may be booked as often as five to eight times a week.

Rather than wait to be called, Lucile promotes herself to assure a continuing series of speaking engagements. She collects names of women's organizations from newspaper announcements, mailing lists, and the telephone directory. Late in the summer she mails a folder describing her crafts to the program chairman for these organizations—PTA groups, church circles, and women's organizations. When a program chairman responds, she supplies a photo showing her crafting a flower arrangement for local publicity. These announcements attract other invitations to speak and her booking calendar quickly fills up, sometimes a month ahead. After two seasons requests flow in regularly because she puts on a good show.

If your craft can be adapted to this specialized marketing technique, develop your speaking ability. Your craft techniques will not

carry the show by itself if your presentation is dull. Learn to dramatize each step in your demonstration, and keep the patter light and
humorous. Unless you have considerable experience, practice your
presentation over and over for friends or in your own classes. A fast-
moving, sometimes humorous lecture must, first of all, be entertaining. Unless you capture and hold the ladies' attention, your commercial at the end falls flat. You invest your time to attract direct
sales, follow-on attendance at classes, and sales in your shop. A half-
hearted, amateurish performance yields few benefits. While this approach does not work for everyone, it can be a powerful sales booster
for the craftsman with a touch of the ham actor in his or her make-
up and a flair for promotion.

Display a varied selection of your crafts—varied in style, design,
size, and price. During your demonstration, show individual pieces as
examples of specific techniques. This way you show variety without
obvious selling. End your talk with a question-and-answer period following your commercial; then invite inspection after the meeting
breaks up. An inexpensive folder or a single sheet describing your
products, kits, lessons, and activities promotes you and your craft
products. Distribute them freely. Attendees who appear the quietest
and ask the fewest questions often turn out to be your best customers.

Demonstrations and talks before women's groups can also be
profitable for crafts that require major equipment and considerable
skill. Ceramics, stitchery, jewelry, and weaving afford entertaining
subjects for talks and open up a custom market for special orders. Include a plug for custom orders in your talk, then distribute order
blanks after a meeting. A weaver, for example, might offer a full selection of colored yarns for custom-finished boleros and capes or wall
hangings. By special order, a customer selects colors, designs, and
size. Or a jeweler indicates in a talk that he designs new mounts for
existing gemstones.

Restaurants and Exhibitions

Popular restaurants experience overloads at peak periods. While
patrons are waiting to be seated, they may as well be examining
crafts and paintings. Innovative restaurants are finding that crafts

and arts offer additional income opportunities. Jewelry, stitchery wall hangings, paintings, mosaics, and driftwood items prove popular. You can follow these details for developing a plan that works for craftsmen with an eye to year-round profits.

Survey the fine restaurants in your city, particularly those outside the downtown areas. Outlying restaurants will usually cater mainly to the dinner trade, and these patrons are the prime prospects. Look for foyer spaces according to your crafts. If you design stitchery wall hangings, look for open wall areas. If you are a jeweler or silversmith, look for spots to mount a glass-covered, locked case. These might be vertical or horizontal—both can be used effectively. Ceramics or pottery will need protected shelf space or a glass-front cabinet. Framed mosaics can be wall mounted.

Call the manager of each potential restaurant for an appointment, preferably between two and five in the afternoon. Bring varied samples of your work according to your craft—three to five framed mosaics or stitchery wall hangings, a chest of jewelry items, and a few smaller pieces of pottery. If you have colored photos of other work mounted in a loose-leaf portfolio, bring those along too. Include any publicity clippings, award certificates, or photos of competition cups or plaques in your portfolio for added credibility. Present your proposal quickly on a business basis. You have these specific pluses going for you—

❖ Crafts present conversation starters for patrons waiting to be seated, thereby reducing the aggravation of waiting. Crafts initiate entertaining discussions and invite comment among patrons. With time on their hands they will inevitably be drawn to examining your work.

❖ A constantly changing "craft show in residence" encourages patrons to return regularly to see what's new in the foyer gallery.

❖ Commissions earned on sales increase the restaurant's profits with little or no investment. You should offer to change the exhibits periodically and to replace sold items with new offerings. The opportunity for the restaurant to earn income from otherwise unproductive floor space can be your most effective selling point. Although the rate is negotiable, a 25 per cent commission is typical for these arrangements. As an individual craftsman, you may settle for 20 to

33⅓ per cent—but seldom for any higher commission. If your crafts are one of a number on display by a club or association, you will be bound by the rules negotiated for all.

Offer to display your crafts on trial first. Your appeal here is "What have you got to lose?" Once on exhibit your crafts will surely create interest and comment among patrons. Sales depend on the class of patrons drawn to the restaurant. Those featuring a lake or seashore location, an outstanding view, or outstanding food will draw patrons able to buy your crafts. You sell by offering your crafts to persons with money. Some restaurants use arts and crafts exhibits as an advertising ploy—"Announcing the works of ——, now on display." You may want to appear at the opening much like a gallery preview.

When a restaurant accepts your plan, select pieces to be displayed consistent with the space allowed. At first a restaurant may allow you only a minimum space. If your crafts are to hang on the wall, arrange them artistically and include a small price tag in a lower corner, usually on a printed card with your name and phone number. The restaurant cashier handles the sale, and the manager turns over your portion of the cash received. If your craft is jewelry, display a range of pieces in a glass-covered case, possibly under the glass counter where checks are paid. A better spot is away from the cash register and well lighted. Individual pieces should be price marked with a tag visible through the glass case. An interested customer asks the hostess or maître d' for permission to see a particular piece. Access to the case must be limited to authorized personnel. Display a neatly hand-painted or lettered sign in the case with your name, address, and telephone number. You may be permitted to leave a stack of your business cards alongside the cash counter. Patrons will, thereby, be encouraged to visit your shop or call for prices on custom work.

Handle restaurant sales similar to sales through a consignment shop (see Chapter 5). Inventory each piece along with the price and a notation of the date first exhibited. Make sure you go over the inventory with the restaurant manager to check prices and to agree on the number of pieces consigned. Ask the manager to sign your copy of the inventory.

Check in with the management regularly to pick up the cash for sales and to replace items sold with new pieces. Keep the display ever changing. Every week you may want to hang new mosaics on the wall or add new pieces to a jewelry display case. Each time you add a new piece or remove a piece that has been on display, update the inventory. A constantly changing exhibit maintains freshness and adds to the conversation value of regular patrons who will begin to look for new additions. A changing exhibit also indicates that pieces are selling.

Restaurants offer only one possibility for specialty outlets. Look to hotel lobbies, bank offices, department store wall areas (particularly where craft materials are sold or in a home furnishings section), private clubs, and office buildings. You may not break into some of these locations as an individual. But if you belong to a local arts and crafts association or co-operative, encourage the group to display a variety of craft works. A bank may not be willing to deal with an individual but will aid an organization.

Close to a hundred paintings, mosaics, and stitchery items are featured along a connecting hallway at the Sahara Tahoe Hotel under the auspices of the South Lake Tahoe Art League. During busy times, a league member "sits" with the display to answer questions and to sell individual pieces. Although theft is a possibility when works are displayed in spaces open to the public, experience indicates few problems when items are large. Jewelry and small crafts need the protection of a glass case in any exhibit.

If you are a member of a craft league or co-operative, initiate a program with businesses in your community. Club management may consider an exhibit as a means of fostering interest in crafts. When a number of craftsmen exhibit, a sponsoring bank or other business may charge no commission, but may not handle sales directly. A group that plans and manages a display or exhibit deducts a 20 to 25 per cent commission on individual sales for expenses.

Special Promotions

Craft shows or displays are gaining popularity at the Christmas season as a promotion for shopping. New covered mall shopping centers offer customers protection from the weather in a main aisleway. Many of the same advantages that accrue to the summer arts and crafts fair boost the sales potential from a special exhibit. Plus—one more! Crowds before Christmas shop in a spending mood, and crafts make ideal gifts. A craft show in a shopping center will normally be sponsored by a craft league or nonprofit association. But, as a member of a nonprofit association, you can sell your own products at normal prices. If you belong to a craftsmen's guild, league, co-operative, or other group, plan far ahead for a Christmas show in a local shopping center by following these steps:

❖ Appoint one of your members to contact the management of the shopping mall. You'll find them receptive to any good idea that will attract customers. Many of the malls organize shows themselves, such as an outdoor living show for trailers and camping gear, boats, imported cars, recreational vehicles, and fashions. Sponsoring a show that costs them nothing, but temporary space affords shopping mall management with a promotable event. Ads paid for by the shopping center herald "Free Craft Exhibits. See craftsmen at work in the ——— Mall."

❖ As a group, offer to staff the exhibit with "Craftsmen in Action." Stage the same attention-getting activities that draw crowds to the summer arts and crafts fairs. Plan an enclosure with the help of the mall management. Bench-high exhibit cases and places for craftsmen to work may alternate with selling areas. The number of craftsmen who may participate and the variety of crafts offered for sale depend on the space available.

❖ Since promotion potential offers the key to gaining space in a mall, emphasize known personalities in your group—craftsmen who have gained a reputation or who can demonstrate wood carving, jewelry handcrafting, or glass blowing. The mall will want to promote the craft show to attract traffic into the store areas. Your co-operation in providing name craftsmen that the public recognizes will help.

❖ Negotiate an even trade without a fee. In exchange for space in a mall, the management may ask for a percentage of gross sales. No more than 20 per cent should be negotiated if craftsmen participate and man the sales areas. A better arrangement is a strict trade—your group stages a craft fair in a mall area in exchange for the opportunity to sell with no cash changing hands.

Some crafts might be barred. If a specialty pot shop operates in the mall, potters might be excluded—too much direct competition. Jewelry craftsmen might be barred if adjoining shops offer handcrafted jewelry as a regular item.

When arranging a holiday craft fair, remember that mall management is looking for an attraction. Consider your show as a crowd-pleasing, Craftsmen-in-Action exhibit—not just a static display of crafts for sale. Action is the key. People are attracted by skilled craftsmen plying their skills and available to answer questions, change a ring size, or sell their own kits and books. Craft kits packaged as gifts sell big when a craftsman demonstrates techniques for using the packaged materials. Christmas craft shows may open as early as a week or two before Thanksgiving and continue at one location throughout the Christmas gift-buying season. Such a show and promotion offer another season for selling beyond the summer festival season.

Gift and Decorator Shows

Industry shows for gift shop buyers and professional decorators offer a huge market for the craft organization or group that can deliver large volumes of production or semiproduction crafts. *Gift and Decorative Accessories* Magazine covers this market exhaustively —details the location and dates of shows where crafts might be exhibited, and notes the organizers where more information may be obtained. Other specialty magazines, such as *Craft, Model and Hobby Industry,* and *Profitable Craft Merchandising* list shows where crafts can be exhibited for sale to volume buyers. Another source for leads is the Chamber of Commerce or Visitors Bureau of the major cities in your area.

Exhibiting at shows can be expensive—$250 to $500 for a space to display your wares. You will need some sort of a catalogue and price list along with typical samples of your work. But your main requirement is the ability to deliver goods in volume. Ordinarily, the industry show offers few opportunities for the individual craftsman.

To participate in an industry show, first contact the director or manager. You will receive a packet of information—booth locations and prices, contract for space, and miscellaneous attendance and other data. Arrangements for shows are completed months ahead, so request information early. Before signing a contract, you should gain some experience by attending several industry shows, preferably the one you are considering. Talk with others exhibiting or actually work with a friend or acquaintance on the floor to gain firsthand experience. Pick up all the information you can before committing yourself.

Institutional Sales

Businesses catering to the public offer a largely untapped market for handcrafts. New motels and hotels furnish luxury accommodations with original oil paintings, lamp bases from one-of-a-kind ceramics, and wall hangings of stitchery or weaving. Institutions buy handcrafts for the same reasons as individuals—to achieve individuality and distinction. Restaurants may also serve delicacies in handcrafted pots to achieve an elegance not attainable any other way. Reaching this market ranges from the difficult to the impossible. But, once sold, one buyer accounts for a huge volume.

Suppose a new international hotel chain begins construction of a multistory modern hotel. Interior designers begin planning room decor and furnishings at about the same time excavators begin digging for the foundation. Not all rooms and suites warrant top-drawer attention. But out of 600 rooms, say, 120 will be furnished luxuriously. That means at least 240, possibly 360 ceramic or carved wood lamp bases will be needed—not all alike. In addition, 120 paintings, framed mosaics, or stitchery hangings will be needed to dress room walls. Designers will be looking for distinctive pieces within their decorating budget. Price will always be a factor. While individuality and a lack of sameness will be specified, the craftsman can develop semiproduction methods to assure freshness and to control costs.

Two avenues lead to sales in the institutional markets. One route is directly through the institution's purchasing staff and the department responsible for decorating and furnishing facilities. If you or a representative of your group can produce the quantity of pieces that will be required, make a frontal attack, beginning with the receptionist at the executive offices. Ask first for the person responsible for buying furnishings. Relate your story that you (and others, if you represent a group) can furnish handcraft quality for close to the same prices as run-of-the-mill production pieces. Photos of typical pieces in a neat portfolio will convince the purchasing officer of your credibility. The next stop may be to review your products and plan with a representative of the decorating staff. Don't expect an on-the-spot decision. In one study an average of eight calls to a large organization's purchasing office was necessary before getting the first order. You may be put off for any number of credible reasons—timing too early or too late for a specific project, decision maker out of town, your original offering impractical, large purchases confirmed only on acceptance of competitive bid proposals, and others. Persistence and an understanding of big business buying methods could lead to a big order. An agent can be a valuable go-between when contacting professional buyers.

The second approach is through major interior decorating consultants who contract to furnish hotels, business offices, restaurants, and other public places. Your contact here is with a principal of the firm. Your reputation as a designer-craftsman pays off in gaining entry to see a designer. Instead of proposing crafts for a specific job, such as the opening of a new resort hotel, offer a line of products and ideas for their application. Suggest ceramic sculptures to carry out the motif for a bar or cabaret, driftwood and things nautical for a restaurant to capture the flavor of an ocean outlook, or a stitchery hanging instead of an abstract painting to complement a reception hall in a modern office building. Any designer worth his salt will create his own ideas of how to use your crafts. Your task is to fire up his imagination, get his creative juices flowing, and to offer a reliable source of handcrafted originals for implementing specific design assignments. Your products will help him to achieve something original and innovative. By helping the designer, you help yourself.

Selling handcrafts in quantity to institutional buyers directly or through designers requires long-range planning. The first contact you make today could pay off next year. Consider institutional sales as a long-range goal—and keep the small, individual sales going in the meantime to maintain a steady cash flow. As one sales organization puts it, "You can starve to death between kills if you hunt only elephants. Keep your eye out for a few rabbits every day as you pursue the elephant."

Executive Gift Market

Industrial selling involves a full palette of techniques that range from outright bribery to more sophisticated influences such as yacht trips, paid fishing jaunts, a night on the town for a purchasing agent and his wife, or a tasteful gift at Christmas time. One item remains prominent on the list—gifts to decision makers. Whole catalogues of potential gifts range from expensive luggage to personalized pen and pencil sets. For the very special person, handcrafted jewelry, ceramics, mosaics, or any of a number of crafts that may be easily shipped offer a guarantee of thoughtfulness and taste. Expect these gifts to trend toward the lower end of your price schedule. Remember, too, that only gifts within the $25 limit are tax deductible as a business expense. To remain under this ceiling, your wholesale price will be limited to no more than $12.50.

If you believe your crafts would make unusual and attractive executive gifts, contact firms that specialize in gift packages early in the year. There will not be a large traffic in this market, but offer the sales organization unique handcrafts. Show examples of varied small pieces and photographs of others. You can find the addresses of firms dealing in executive gifts listed in the classified telephone directory under "Advertising Specialties." Again, long-range planning is essential. Decisions on which lines to offer are usually made in spring or early summer. You may be asked to supply pieces for shipment as early as September.

Charity Fund-raising Bazaars

In the two months before Christmas, gift and charity bazaars spring up like toadstools in the damp shade. Many of these bazaars sell only gifts crafted by members as donations to raise money for some worthy cause. These will not interest you as a selling craftsman. Other bazaars organize to sell crafts on consignment, and you can benefit because the commission on sales runs as low as 20 per cent. Charity shops and gift bazaars attract considerable attention because newspapers devote space to photos of prominent individuals in their role as organizers of charity functions. Members of the sponsoring organizations receive flyers. Bazaar announcements receive prominent space in monthly newsletters. Members are encouraged to buy Christmas gifts from the shop to aid charity goals. Costs for operating such shops are minimal because members donate their time.

As a craftsman you can participate in seasonal charity bazaars the same as any other consignment shop. Watch for announcements in local newspapers, particularly the neighborhood shoppers. If you happen to know the woman's editor of your local newspaper, ask her for contacts. Search through the files of newspapers during a previous holiday season for organizations sponsoring bazaars the previous year. Over several years you can develop a list of organizations who sponsor bazaars and pick the best ones (those that generate volume sales at low commission). Contact the organization by calling the president. Ask for the name of the chairman responsible for the bazaar. Planning begins in early fall for Christmas sales, so don't wait until Thanksgiving to begin your search.

Another charity outlet—hospital gift shops operated by an auxiliary of the hospital association. Visit the hospital and ask at the shop who is responsible for selecting gifts offered, and go on from there. Inexpensive paper crafts, jewelry, needlework, stitchery in frames or for hangings, and small ceramics for flower vases or plants are popular items in hospital shops. These shops offer a market throughout the year and sell crafts on consignment only—usually with only a small commission in the 20–30 per cent range.

Door-to-Door Selling

Would you believe a specialty market exists through door-to-door selling? Paintings were sold door-to-door at the rate of $500/week in one case. The *modus operandi* is simple. Take out a peddler's license or pay for a resale permit to assure not being picked up by local police. Then, haul your crafts from one house to another. Middle-class neighborhoods appear to offer the best hunting ground for sales. It's a risky business that demands nerve, persistence, and an ability to remain optimistic in the face of slammed doors and brusque brushoffs. But for the door-to-door craftsman-salesman, the payoff can be fantastic. If you decide to introduce this old sales technique to the craft field, adapt some of the techniques that paid off for the artist:

❖ Items in a medium price range.
❖ Designs that build on dreams or add "class" to a living room, such as unique impulse ceramics, jewelry, or stitchery.
❖ Sales for cash or checks.

Door-to-door selling of crafts is likely to pay off in affluent neighborhoods with young families on their way up. The uniqueness of your approach will usually gain you a hearing. From that point on, your crafts and your salesmanship make the difference.

Chapter 5

SELLING WHOLESALE OR ON
CONSIGNMENT

Suppose you really dislike selling—meeting the public—or think marketing is crass, unrewarding. You really prefer designing and creating —doing what you do best. Then, separating creative functions from marketing makes uncommonly good sense for you. Many highly creative craftsmen and artists exhibit little talent or interest in reporting sales taxes, maintaining inventory valuations, renting a store, and hiring help for the times they can't be on hand personally. If you're one of them, you should probably turn over the marketing of your crafts to experts.

How do you go about marketing your craft products through someone else? First, recognize that marketing is an economic activity —shop owners expect to make a profit on their sales of your crafts. Second, recognize the difference between marketing your crafts and marketing yourself. More than a slight distinction separates these two ideas, as you discovered in Chapter 2. Two primary methods for selling crafts are wholesale and consignment selling.

Wholesale vs. Consignment Selling

You'll find vocal proponents for both wholesale and consignment selling. Both methods are in wide and general use throughout the United States and in many other countries. Basically, these are the differences, advantages, and disadvantages of each system:

Price—You, as the craftsman, pocket less of the retail sales price of a craft article when sold wholesale than when sold on consignment.

A common markup for wholesale trade is 50 per cent of the retail price. The same markup figured on cost amounts to 100 per cent (see Chapter 3—Pricing). You should know the difference, but markup figures in the remaining parts of this chapter and book represent a percentage of the retail price. Consignment shops selling on consignment may take as much as a 40 per cent markup. The usual markup is one third or 33⅓ per cent. Some shops may take 25 or even as little as 20 per cent. The remainder goes to you, the craftsman. Actual retail sales price of the crafts should be similar whether you sell wholesale or on consignment. Therefore, selling on consignment at 33⅓ or 25 per cent markups yields more cash to you *when sold*. So, consider timing.

Timing—When you sell wholesale, you receive your money immediately or up to thirty or sixty days later if you extend trade credit (see Chapter 12). In exchange for a lower wholesale price (higher markup), you receive the full amount immediately or on credit terms. When selling on consignment, you receive your cut of the retail price when and if your work actually sells. Most well-run consignment shops pay craftsmen at the end of each month for sales during that month. A piece unsold on display for months remains part of your capital. Your time and money spent for materials remain invested while the item languishes. Most craft shops will return a piece that does not sell within their time limit—perhaps three months, possibly up to six or eight months. Like most retail establishments, consignment shops keep their stock turning over, new things coming in and selling, older nonselling items moving out. If your goods do not move, you will be asked to remove them, usually at your expense.

Volume—How much of your production a specific shop may sell depends very little on whether the shop buys wholesale or sells on consignment. You may find it profitable to display your crafts in a number of shops on consignment to increase volume rather than sell wholesale to one or only a few stores. Volume sales depend on your productivity—not how the stock is acquired.

Marketing—Your marketing strategy depends on whether your production is keyed to large volume or fewer individually designed pieces. Large production craft shops usually sell wholesale through trade shows or by hiring a salesman or representative. A large producer may also market to a number of wholesale outlets through an agent or on consignment through the mail (see Chapter 7). Aside from these large-scale operations, most craftsmen market their goods by personally showing their crafts to galleries, gift-shop owners, and craft outlets operated by charity or fund-raising organizations. As noted in Chapter 3, your pricing must allow for such selling activities. Galleries screen offerings, using a variety of criteria, but the personal taste of the owner predominates. Your reputation as a designer, artist, or craftsman influences gallery operators as much as their perceived quality of your work. Galleries usually sell on consignment only. Juried outlets accept only those crafts that pass the scrutiny of a review board of acknowledged peer designer craftsmen. To market through such a large volume shop, a designer craftsman must offer unique, stylishly designed, original crafts. Finding the best marketing approach to shops and galleries requires considerable research, trial and error, and creative thinking. *Artisan Crafts* publishes a "Guide to the Craft World" that offers a starting place.

Record Keeping—Selling wholesale simplifies record keeping—one major benefit. When you sell wholesale for cash, the transaction is completed in a simple transfer of title. Record keeping becomes more complicated if you must set up an accounts receivable ledger and follow up with credit billing. Selling on consignment requires detailed, though not elaborate, records of transactions by piece or lot. Since you receive no payment until a piece is sold, you must maintain an inventory of pieces by location and keep that inventory up to date as sales and payments are made. A consignment-sale record-keeping system is detailed later in this chapter.

Profitability—Businessmen refer to the payoff as "the bottom line." After all costs are paid, time allocations for marketing and distribution assessed, and prices for wholesale matched against the take from consignment sales, the resulting payoff or bottom line represents your total profitability. If your skills permit fast, volume production of individually designed pieces, you may find wholesale selling more profitable because you can spend more hours producing at your bench. But if you prize individual creative design, you may gain more by selling on consignment through a gallery that trades on individuality and designer reputation. No rigid rules or pat formulas will simplify this decision for you. Instead, you must examine alternatives and devise your own marketing strategy, possibly after consulting with potential sources of information as detailed in Chapter 12. Following are proved ideas for selling your craft products either wholesale or on consignment:

Wholesale Selling

When you sell wholesale, title to your crafts changes hands just as in a retail sale. A quantity buyer for a store or other outlet accepts the risk that your craft goods will sell and pays for them outright. Most sales at wholesale are shipped and billed for later payment. While extending credit to wholesale buyers is an accepted practice, learn early to protect yourself against poor credit risks as detailed in Chapter 12.

Pricing can be critical when producing for the wholesale market, as the store may disagree with your valuations. And—the store buyer still has the last word. If a buyer believes he cannot sell your crafts at a price that will generate a profit for him, he won't buy and you have no sale.

Buyers are the strong men and women in the marketing chain. Although you must sell your products to a wholesale buyer as you would directly to a consumer, two differences will be readily apparent:

First, wholesale buyers are much more knowledgeable and objective than buyers in retail outlets. They buy to sell, not to use.

Second, a few good wholesale outlets can commit your total production capacity. One of the problems of marketing through wholesale channels is being able to deliver enough goods of the quality, variety, and craftsmanship desired by the buyer without turning your shop into an assembly line.

Selling successfully at wholesale to gift, home furnishings, or craft store buyers typically runs like this: You show samples of your work to a buyer. Depending on the size of the store, you may need to call ahead for an appointment. On a first contact, the buyer will examine the design and workmanship in great detail. He or she may consult with one or more sales persons during or after the initial contact. The buyer may ask you to leave selected samples for study and review by a buyers' group. The buyer surveys the variety and volume of similar goods already in the store. He may consult his records to check on sales. He will most certainly compare the size, finish, quality of construction, and uniqueness of design of your products with those already for sale in his shop. He mentally tabs sales and prices of goods with which he is already familiar. All of these activities precede any discussion of price.

A shrewd buyer never tells you first what he will pay for your goods. He will ask you to set a price for your work. If you have completed your marketing homework, you will know current market prices for goods like yours. You should state your prices precisely and be prepared to stand relatively firm—with possibly a little room left for negotiating. Don't, under any circumstances, respond to the buyer's question about price with a question like "Well, what do you think is a fair price?" Or, "I don't really know. What can you sell my pieces for?" Such remarks brand you as a rank amateur. The buyer's job is to buy goods the shop can sell at a profit—not to help you price your goods.

If your price quotation fits a range of the shop's sales pattern, bargaining will continue. If you haven't already determined the price range, you shouldn't be talking with the buyer. If you price your goods out of selling range compared to goods already being sold in the shop, you lose a sale. If you're close, the buyer may extend a counteroffer at a lower price. If the counteroffer falls above your "last-ditch" price, you can accept. For a first sale you may agree to a lower price than you expect to receive later. Delivery and purchase terms are negotiated quickly after the price is agreed to. An initial order may be small to permit the shop to test the market for your goods among their customers. A buyer will minimize risk with a new and untried supplier by selecting one or only a few sample items.

Later sales depend entirely on how quickly your first order moves out to customers. If your goods appeal to the shop's clientele, you can count on continuing orders. If your crafts do not sell, you may exercise two options: First, write off that shop as an outlet for your goods. You and the buyer simply misjudged the market. Second, offer to exchange the goods in stock for other articles of equal value. Your products might not sell in Store A, but sell readily in Store B with its different image and clientele. If your replacement stock sells, you have learned the kind of articles to promote through that store.

Variations on the theme of selling wholesale come in all shades. Two designers, Mel Alford and Charles Pettibone, produce leather purses, belts, and hangings in strikingly original designs. Their loosely organized partnership functions under the simple name—Leather. The two craftsmen sell from a van workshop loaded with their work. They use the van as a rolling showroom and appear at their regular customers' shops unannounced at irregular intervals. At a typical stop, Mel and Chuck load an armful of their work from the van and stride into the shop. Or if they have sold the store before, the buyer usually visits the van parked in an alley or on the street to examine a greater variety of pieces.

Leather's goods sell at a relatively fast clip considering they move at the high end of the price range. A few hangings have sold for prices around $200. Purses may sell for $39.95 to $119.50. Occasionally a buyer attempts to buy a substantial part of their inventory because he has sold out completely. Leather refrains from large-scale selling to one outlet, preferring instead to spread their work around in a variety of locations.

If the buyer has no experience with Leather's goods, he examines the design and workmanship in great detail. Unless he is new in the business, he will have seen examples of Leather's pieces in craft shows or on competitors' shelves. Bargaining shifts to price quickly. All of the samples exhibited are marked with a fixed price and the two partners no longer haggle. Although they work together, each of the two craftsmen sells his own work and keeps his own books. A purchase by a shop owner may call for two checks if he buys from both Mel and Charles. Further, they sell for cash only—delivering the goods from their van on the spot and picking up their check before they leave.

The two Leather designers work on a batch basis. When they have filled their van with finished pieces, they take off on a selling trip and stay on the road until their stock is gone. Then they return to their shop to design and craft a new load of articles. By opening up new outlets and maintaining a controlled scarcity of their goods, they can keep their prices relatively high. Further, the loss of a single outlet offers no threat to their continuing income.

Employing an agent gets you into wholesale selling through another route. An agent supplies pricing expertise, contacts buyers for several craftsman-producers, checks credit, arranges financing on occasion, and may offer suggestions on design and materials. An agent is a selling specialist whether in real estate, nuclear engineering, or crafts. As a go-between, an agent must know where specific kinds of crafts sell and craftsmen capable of producing salable crafts for those outlets are working. Since an agent earns a commission only when he or she sells something, acquiring an agent can be a problem. You need an agent most when you are trying to establish yourself as a producing designer craftsman. But few agents will take on a beginner. After you have established a number of outlets and proved your capability, you might not need an agent. At that stage an agent will be interested in representing you.

An agent sells only on a wholesale basis, and the usual commission amounts to 15 per cent of the wholesale price. With a $1.00 retail price and a wholesale price of $.50, an agent's commission amounts to 15 per cent of $.50 or $.07½, leaving the craftsman with $.42½. If you manage your time and design crafts that can be produced on a quantity basis, an agent can more than earn his commission. With more time at your bench, you can generate more goods for sale. Separating production from selling functions follows basic economics of work specialization. You, as the designer craftsman, can work at your specialty, the agent works at his. As long as the agent sells only on commission, you pay his fee only when he produces.

An agent will usually sell from a sample kit. If you are a silversmith, you would design and produce one of each kind of ring, pendant, bracelet, and other designs. The agent shows your samples and takes orders. He will contact buyers, take orders for specific items, and forward the orders to you for production and delivery according to a schedule. If a ring is ordered, it will be ordered in a specific size. If a pendant is available in different sizes or fitted with various chains, each option will be specified. Prices will be stated according to a price list you both agree on. You bill the customer direct with a copy to the agent. The customer will ordinarily pay you directly, but the agent may receive payments, deduct his commission, and send the remainder on to you. Note that the agent does not buy the goods or take title from you. If the agent bought the goods for resale, you would charge wholesale prices.

You and the agent must agree on credit terms and handling of payments. For example, you might agree to ship jewelry to a store only if payments are received within 45 days of shipment—possibly 60 days with the second 30 days subject to a 1 or 1½ per cent service charge. Shipments would be made up to a credit limit. For new accounts the credit limit would be set relatively low. Once a satisfactory payment pattern is established, the credit limit could be raised in stages. One of an agent's responsibilities is to check out buyers' credit, but you, not he, are the loser if the store doesn't pay. Thus, you will need to control shipments only to credit-worthy customers.

A contract detailing your working arrangements, credit limits, commission schedule, and minimum volumes will prevent misunderstandings between you and the agent. Since a contract is a two-way street, you should insist on a minimum volume of sales. That is, the agent must agree to bring in a minimum volume of sales; otherwise, you are free to cancel the contract on 30-day notice. The minimum volume can begin low for the first year, then increase according to your production capability and the agent's sales ability. Contract dissolution terms should also be specified. Before signing any contract, review all terms with your attorney.

How do you find an agent? How do you find an agent who will sell a satisfactory volume of your crafts? Since reputable agents do not advertise, you must search them out. A buyer at a store, associates who now are using an agent for a noncompeting craft, or contacts through a craft co-op or fair can produce names of potential agents. An agent may contact you through a referral from a store buyer if you are selling regularly. You could contact the Chamber of Commerce in your area to determine if there is a local group of manufacturer's representatives (agents) or a salesman's organization. An inquiry to such an organization could lead to an agent who specializes in crafts. Ordinarily, you must take the first step to find an agent and then sell him or her on representing you. Finding the right agent can be a frustrating and often lengthy search. There's little point in tying up with a poor one, and the good ones are already busy.

Hiring your own salesman differs from contracting with an agent. As an independent businessman, the agent may represent several craftsmen (in noncompeting crafts) plus other manufacturers. The agent pays all of his own expenses and earns commissions on sales.

He pays his own taxes and is not entitled to employee benefits. A salesman, on the other hand, is an employee who brings with him all of his problems and costs. An employee may be paid on commission, but generally he will be paid a draw against commissions, meaning an early payment for expenses and salary. As your own employee he will sell only your goods. Thus, your production must be large enough to support a commission schedule that permits the salesman to earn a satisfactory salary. Direct salesmen are, however, more controllable and their attention will not be diverted by other lines. Generally, a business must employ a number of producing craftsmen turning out a substantial volume of goods to warrant hiring a full-time salesman. But if your business grows, your own salesman could pay off better than an agent who assumes more risks and takes a higher percentage of gross sales.

Consignment Selling

Despite its many drawbacks, consignment selling continues as the predominant form of marketing for individual craftsmen. Boutiques, galleries, fund-raising groups, and associations of craftsmen suffer one common malady—lack of capital. A serious lack of management know-how also afflicts many of these amateur sales outlets. From your point of view as a producing craftsman, you stand to gain a higher price for your work, but you will have to wait to pick up the cash. When you consign your craftwork to an outlet, you retain title until your work sells. You invest the value of your completed work in the shop's inventory. In exchange for your investment in its inventory and co-operation in waiting to be paid, the shop undertakes a varied marketing campaign. The shop picks up the tab for advertising, shop rent, promotion expense, and salaries of sales personnel. A consignment shop profits only when it sells your goods and that of other craftsmen represented among their stock. By selling on consignment, a shop can afford to acquire a larger and more varied inventory than if it had to buy at wholesale prices.

The Northwest Craft Center (NCC) on the grounds of the Seattle Center operates as a nonprofit corporation organized by and run for the benefit of designer craftsmen in the Pacific Northwest. The NCC functions in a building left from the Seattle World's Fair of

1962 and affords a show place for crafts of all kinds in a central location frequented by out-of-town visitors. The work of more than two hundred individual craftsmen is artistically displayed by a professional staff. Crafts displayed span a wide price and size range from contemporary furniture to ceramic sculpture to sterling silver rings. Pottery and ceramics abound in the shop, reflecting the area's interest in pottery and the many fine local potters. Candles, wall hangings of macramé, wood cutouts, handwoven ties, stitchery hangings, hand-blocked stationery, and prints fill the bright, gay shop. The city of Seattle permits the shop to pay rent as a percentage of its gross sales because the Craft Center provides a "free show" for visitors. Tourists "discover" the shop in their tour of the Center and spend hours browsing among the shop's crafts.

The Northwest Craft Center accepts crafts for sale only on consignment and takes a 40 per cent commission. A board of five trustees, all active and producing craftsmen, control the corporation. As craftsmen, the board understands the needs of other craftsmen and insists on regular monthly payments for crafts sold during the past thirty days. Checks go out regularly and on time to selling craftsmen. While the 40 per cent "take" exceeds many shops' commission schedules, the volume of sales through the NCC provides a big market for producing craftsmen. One potter averages about $10,000 in sales year in and year out. Craftsmen from all over the Puget Sound region are among the regulars at the NCC.

All crafts on display at the Northwest Craft Center must first pass muster from a jury of craftsmen. After preliminary screening, a review board judges a new craftsman's work on the basis of originality in design, quality of craftsmanship, technique, consistency, and quantity of work offered. When a craftsman's work is accepted for display, the Center may schedule an exhibit or "one-man show." Sometimes the work of two or three craftsmen will be featured in a special showing. During the special show, usually extending over four weeks, the works of the featured craftsmen occupy a special location and are displayed with a distinctive flair. Scheduling a show affords the Center an opportunity to promote the work of the craftsmen and continues to call attention to the Northwest Craft Center.

The White Whale operates on a completely different scale than

1. Bellevue Arts and Crafts Fair visitors ogle crafts in variety of media in open shopping square in Bellevue, Washington. Constant vigilance prevents shoplifting of small ceramic objects. Note hanging ceramic necklaces from "tree" at right. A wide variety of crafts for sale aids sales. Craftsmen often sell a third to half their year's production at fairs. (Photo: *Doug Wilson*)

2. Wooden toys fascinate the younger crowd at arts and crafts fair booth. Youngsters can be persuasive in opening parents' pocketbooks to build sales volume. (Photo: *Doug Wilson*)

3.   Maintaining production during quiet periods reduces time investment when selling at crafts fairs. Small price dot in corner of individual items encourages sales.
(Photo: *Doug Wilson*)

4.   Artists in action never fail to attract attention. Popular attraction at crafts fairs is potter working at portable wheel. (Photo: *Doug Wilson*)

5.   Handcrafted silver jewelry attracts attention as a favorite at open-air craft fairs. (Photo: *Doug Wilson*)

the Northwest Craft Center. The White Whale is a small gallery located far off the beaten track in the tiny art colony and fishing village of Gig Harbor, Washington. The shop is small, uncrowded, and overlooks a dock mooring many small boats visible through an enormous picture window. Paintings, sculpture, ceramics, and a great variety of handcrafted jewelry are attractively displayed in the shop. The work of local Gig Harbor craftsmen occupy much of the space, but craftsmen from both Seattle and Tacoma are also represented among the carefully selected offerings on display.

Carole Chalk, owner and prime mover at the Whale, operates her gallery much like the Northwest Craft Center—but in miniature and with a number of small differences. First, The White Whale is a profit-making establishment, at least by intent. Second, artists and craftsmen give up a third of the retail price on their consignment sales. Third, to stimulate traffic at its out-of-the-way location, Carole actively promotes both the shop and the craftsmen whose work is displayed.

Promotion, as detailed in Chapter 2, is the key to building traffic of the right kind. "The right kind," as Carole Chalk phrases it, "are those who come to buy. We mail regular monthly bulletins to our list of previous buyers and others who have evidenced a sincere interest in the gallery," she reports. The bulletins are tastefully designed by Carole's husband, Earl Chalk, a commercial artist. Showings of one or two artists or craftsmen are featured each month. To kick off the showing, Carole schedules a preview, usually on a Thursday afternoon—"to keep the casual crowd down to a minimum." The artist or craftsman whose work is being featured usually appears at the preview, and refreshments are served, sometimes champagne. Sales at a preview often approach the $1,000 mark and get the month's sales off to a flying start. Invited to the previews are the newspaper reporters who monitor the local craft scene for their papers' readers. So, Carole taps another opportunity for publicity.

Craftsmen interested in selling to galleries must:

❖ Produce crafts original in design and skillfully crafted with professional quality.

❖ Display craft products for sale with enough variety and in sufficient quantity to span a wide price range. A silversmith might, for example, display thirty to sixty individual pieces in a size and price range that would interest a variety of potential buyers.

❖ Have established some reputation for their work in the area. Your chances of being featured are greater if people know you or know your work. If you have established a reputation, your work will draw more potential buyers into the gallery than an unknown. Your standing in the community and your reputation as a craftsman mean dollars in your pocket as well as dollars in the till at the gallery.

Nearly all galleries sell crafts on display. Privately endowed and public galleries that display outstanding works for the public's enlightenment may not sell directly. University, city, and state galleries feature shows of outstanding master craftsmen as well as the work of current designer craftsmen. Although you might not sell your crafts directly from such displays, the exposure your work receives from these public galleries enhances your reputation and can be most helpful in furthering acceptance of your work by the galleries that do sell.

Recent years have seen the emergence of shops and galleries that open seasonally. The Christmas season is a favorite. The Country Mouse is such a shop. It began by opening the first week of November and closing at the end of December. Now it is open all year. The Country Mouse operates with two objectives—to provide an outlet for the work of local craftsmen and to offer a source of handcrafted items in great variety for shoppers in the area. The Mouse affords an alternative for shoppers sated from looking at slickly manufactured goods.

Each room of an old house functions as a showcase built around antiques doing double duty as display cases for stuffed toys and doll clothes, quilts, woven articles, artificial flowers, stationery, jewelry, crockery, candles, and sewn crafts. Where possible each of the crafts relates to its normal environment—quilts in a bedroom, hand-woven place mats in a dining room, and crocheted or embroidered hot pads hanging in the kitchen.

Opportunities for the craftsman to sell his or her work through a seasonal shop are considerably greater than through the gallery route. The Country Mouse advertises for and actively solicits for-sale articles from craftsmen in the area. The Mouse sells only on consign-

Fig. 4: Consignment Sales Record

Shop Name _____

Sales Commission, per cent _____

Item Identification	Date Shipped	Date Acknowl-edged	Retail Price	Net Price	Sold		Date Returned	Remarks
					Date	Paid		

ment. Items offered for sale must be expertly crafted and salable. Otherwise, there are few limitations. A gift shop such as the Mouse accepts many more small items sewn, woven, knitted, or crocheted than galleries that prefer ceramics, wood carvings, silver and gold jewelry, and furniture. Handcrafted knickknacks would be acceptable in a seasonal shop but not in a gallery.

Record Keeping can be a drag, but you must keep track of your craftwork out on consignment. The simple Consignment Sales Record shown in Fig. 4 includes the important elements of:

❖ Identification—Each piece or collection of pieces to be sold as a unit must be positively identified with words or code number. Don't attempt to group several pieces to be displayed at one shop as a single entry. Otherwise, when some pieces sell and others are returned, you lose control of individual pieces. A potter might code a medium-size weed pot to be sold individually. He might also code a group of four matched coffee mugs as one unit to be sold together.

❖ Shipment data—The date each piece was shipped or delivered should be marked along with the consignee shop name. Acknowledgment of receipt should be noted on the record sheet. Keep a separate record sheet for each shop.

❖ Price data—Note the intended retail price for each piece and your net price. If you agree to reduce the price after a specified time, note that information in the remarks column.

❖ Sales data—Two items need to be recorded for pieces sold. Note the date sold or the date you were notified the item sold. Note also the date and amount of money received. For some shops these dates will be the same.

❖ Returned data—Note the date any returned goods are received. Under "Remarks" note any item of interest, possible damage, or shop comment on why the piece didn't sell.

Analysis of regular entries in your Consignment Sales Record helps you determine which items are selling, which shops promote and sell your pieces, and when payment can be expected for items sold. Frequently, a shop will pay for items sold at the same time you are advised of the sale. Often a shop will call for additional pieces when stock is depleted through sales. Ask for data to complete the sales columns in your record at that time.

At least once and preferably twice a year, you should reconcile your inventory record with records at the consignment shop. Send a listing of items you show as shipped, but not returned or paid for. The shop should physically check to see that the items you show in their possession are actually there. Any differences should be clarified. Either the shop should pay for the items or show a record of having paid previously or having returned the items. Reconciling records is easier if you do it often and regularly.

One caution on payment: Some consignment shops are notoriously poor payers and some may never pay for goods sold. A shop that opens and accepts crafts for sale may operate for a few months and then close due to poor sales. Cash received for goods sold while the shop was open paid the rent, light bill, and other necessities, possibly cash to the owner for living expenses. But when the shop closes, the cash is gone and none is left to pay the craftsmen whose works were sold. Other shops may simply delay paying craftsmen until months after a sale.

You can guard against the nonpaying or slow-paying consignment shop by one or all of the following:

❖ Ask the shop owner for the names of other craftsmen whose work is being sold in the shop. Then, call the craftsmen and ask frankly about the shop's payment record.

❖ Check the records of the Attorney General's office, the Better Business Bureau, local Credit Bureau, and the Small Claims Court. Any record of activity at these agencies should alert you to a problem.

❖ Ask the shop owner for credit references and check them out by telephone. Also, ask around among your friends and fellow craftsmen for references or information about the payment record of the shop. Get more than one opinion if possible.

❖ Finally, when in doubt, consign only a limited number of items to a shop and await results. If the owner pays promptly for crafts sold, you can extend your commitment by degrees.

Many craftsmen are so eager to display and sell their work they forget about being paid. When you consign your work to a shop, you extend credit to that shop equal to the consignment value of your work. Some consignment shops operate what amounts to a racket.

They never intend to pay the craftsman for his work and fend off requests for payment by one ruse after another until the craftsman gives up in frustration. Continued operation of such shops depends on the operator's ability to attract work from new and gullible craftsmen who are not aware of the shop's nonpaying policy. You avoid these shops and this problem when you investigate the shop.

Joining a local craft organization can aid you as an individual craftsman in at least three ways:

❖ You gain the collected information about various shops and galleries open to the individual craftsman as a sales outlet. Someone in the group will likely know about a shop that doesn't pay, for example.

❖ You gain the clout of an organization in collecting from a nonpaying or slow-paying shop owner.

❖ You gain an opportunity to become known, to participate in shows, and to swap information about selling techniques, price schedules, and group publicity.

Sources of More Information

Craft shops and galleries selling on consignment abound in nearly every community. You can locate potential outlets for your crafts by examining the visual arts section of your local newspaper, particularly the Friday and Sunday editions. Watch the society sections too for charity shops and bazaars. Local outlets are often listed in monthly program listings issued by one or more of the FM radio stations and weekly bulletins in hotels and restaurants aimed at out-of-town visitors. If you live in California, you may join the Consumers Cooperative of Berkeley and sell through their arts and crafts co-op.

Nationally, the American Crafts Council, 44 West 53rd Street, New York, New York 10019, issues a list of outlets in their *Craft Shops/Galleries USA* booklet. Shops and galleries are coded to indicate their sales policy—buy wholesale or sell on consignment only, or both.

Artisan Crafts (address is listed in the Appendix) publishes two sources of information for craftsmen interested in selling their work. It publishes a magazine every quarter with selected information on a variety of craft interests, including stores, shops, and galleries looking for sale items. The same organization operates "The Handcrafts Registry," a special marketing service for subscribers of *Artisan Crafts*. The "Registry" maintains lists of shops interested in acquiring crafts for sale, usually on consignment.

Chapter 6

SELLING YOUR CRAFTS IN YOUR
OWN RETAIL SHOP

Persistent in the dreams of many craftsmen is a studio, gallery, or retail shop of their own. In this dream a craftsman sells his own creations produced at a bench in the shop. Usually the dream studio is
located in a tourist area, such as Ghirardelli Square in San Francisco
or on a shopping avenue in Palm Beach.

Two motives prompt the craftsman to dream of his own studio.
One's name on a restrained sign over the door or on the window may
generate psychic income or satisfy a need for recognition and
confirmation of his self-esteem. More common is the craftsman's
desire to retain a larger share of the retail price of his crafts. Division
of the economic pie, as defined in Chapter 3, appears to favor
others in the distribution chain from craft bench to retail buyer.
That part of the price destined for the retail shop tempts the craftsman mightily.

The marketplace exerts frighteningly efficient discipline. If operating one's own retail shop were as practical and desirable as it might
seem to the individual craftsman, there would be more of them. But
brutal economic realities limit the combination crafts producing
studio-retail shop to those operated by a few individual craftsmen
who also understand marketing. The business skills of management
in marketing, accounting, and purchasing seldom reside in the same
person in company with creative design and execution skills of the
master craftsman.

Most retail crafts shops depend on other activities to sustain their
financial health. As shown in other chapters retail shops often offer

instruction, sell equipment and materials, offer the craft products of other craftsmen, or function as an outlet for seconds. Individual craftsmen who sell all or most of their own crafts at retail prices usually sell from home studios where overhead costs are minimal. Their success depends on personal reputation, contacts with customers at craft fairs, specialized advertising and promotion, or some other innovative marketing ploy that attracts customers.

Jane Wherrette of Mercer Island, Washington, and Puerto Vallarta, Mexico, is one of those who combines craft artistry with marketing skill. She sells most of the pottery she can find time to shape and fire at full retail prices out of her tiny studio built onto her home as an afterthought addition. She sells her soup tureens, covered casseroles, candy jars, lamp bases, planter pots, and the uniquely individual hangings that are unmistakably Wherrette in response to a built-up demand that began when she first switched from painting to clay.

Jane now makes her living through sales of her exquisitely decorated, one-of-a-kind designer pieces. She works furiously, up to eighteen hours a day, during summer and fall. Then she takes off for Mexico to assuage a chronic sinus condition.

Prices for Jane's work range from $25 for a small casserole to $200 or more for an original lamp base with peekaboo cutouts. While she is reluctant to discuss total income, her six months' efforts at wheel and kiln net her enough to live comfortably and put her two girls through college. A prime reason for her ability to generate a good income is her direct sales to customers.

"Oh, you've got a Wherrette," is a familiar exclamation among crafts-conscious women around Seattle. Her work is recognized instantly even though every piece is different—in shape, color, or decoration. Colors trend toward subtle blues and greens with just a spice of red for accent. Pots may be glazed with intricate decorative designs painstakingly applied with brush or carved with small scalpels or dish-shaped tools. Many of her works include sculptured primitive faces in three dimensions.

Most Wherrette pieces serve functionally. While potters and ceramicists debate the issue of function vs. art, Jane feels strongly about seeing her pottery in use. All of her cookware, such as casserole dishes, is ovenproof and fired at high temperatures. Designs lean heavily on primitive art. Alongside her studio she keeps a well-thumbed library of books on art that began with cave drawings and Indian petroglyphs. Many of her pieces are now created to special order from previous customers or their friends.

How does a potter reach Jane's position of selling her entire output, most of it at full retail prices, from her own studio? The path Jane followed is a familiar one for successful, selling craftsmen. Basically, the plan breaks into these successive phases:

❖ "Find a unique style that pleases you," Jane advises. "If your work is not pleasing and rewarding to you, how can you expect to promote and sell it with enthusiasm and sincerity?" She emphasizes the creative quality of unique design.

❖ "Enter every competition, show, fair, gallery exhibition, or juried market available to you." When Jane was satisfied with her designs, she entered competitions. Her creative, functional designs won prizes in numerous shows due to her unusual style and colors. Further, her work won prizes at the nationally recognized Bellevue Arts and Crafts Fair in Washington. These successes led to her first "one-woman" show at the Collector's Gallery. As one step inevitably leads to another, exhibitions followed in the Dave Hall and Henry Art Galleries. Her work was featured as part of a personal article in the *Seattle Times*. As her reputation grew, so did sales.

❖ "Gain wide visibility for your work through galleries and craft outlets," she recommends. When Jane turned professional and moved out of the hobby class, she cultivated various craft outlets—the Crockery Shed, PANACA, and The Little Gallery at Frederick & Nelson, a department store in Seattle. Summers she traveled the festival circuit displaying her wares, sold directly to customers, and took orders for special pieces to be delivered later.

❖ "Develop your own retail store if this is your bent. It's a matter of economics," she says. "When I sell from my own studio, I get full price for my work. Consignment sales through most of the other outlets net me only two thirds of the sale price. When time limits how much I can make, I want full price.

❖ "Teach classes in an organized program, such as a school system's adult education program or the YMCA, as I did," Jane continues. (See Chapter 8.) "On the road to your own retail shop, teaching helps to broaden your range of contacts for current or future sales."

Retail Store Operation

Few craftsmen operate their own retail shop profitably because they dislike selling. Those who succeed understand common business functions. Few craftsmen willingly spend the time necessary to worry through the details of operating a store.

Successful craft shops or galleries sell the work of many craftsmen. Such a division of functions allows the craftsman to spend more time at his bench doing what he or she is uniquely qualified to do best. The retail shop owner, on the other hand, spends his time selling to customers, accounting for sales and expenses, advertising, buying, and the multitude of other functions apart from creative crafting.

Jane Wherrette minimizes selling time because customers now seek her out or order by telephone, so she spends a minimum of her time in customer contacts. Even with her small-scale operation, Jane spends about 15 per cent of her work schedule at selling. One of her marketing ploys for concentrating selling time into one segment to minimize interruptions is the "seconds" sale.

Like many potters, Jane occasionally finds pieces that fail to measure up to her standard of quality. And once a piece is fired, that's it. Either she breaks it up for scrap—or sells it as a second. You too can profit from special sales extending over one or two days.

Look at the economics of selling seconds at reduced prices. If you sell your pots at wholesale, you receive 50 per cent of retail. On consignment, the usual commission is around one third. Therefore, you can sell your seconds at one third off from your own studio—and still net the same return as for perfect pots sold through normal channels. Here's how Jane Wherrette cashes in on her seconds:

Jane sets aside those pieces that do not meet her strict standards. Over a normal season, she may collect two or three dozen pieces that she classifies as seconds. When she's ready, she mails a card to former customers and advertises in the classified section of a local newspaper. Total expenses usually run to less than $25. Yet, her studio is swamped with customers eager to buy a Wherrette at less than the going rate in the shops.

Seconds sales offer yet another advantage for Jane—she also sells her perfect pots at full retail prices. When a customer cannot find a second to her liking, she will be disappointed. Having already made the effort to locate Jane's out-of-the-way studio, the customer looks at her regular selection and will often buy a piece at full price. Offering seconds appeals to the bargain hunters, but shoppers can be enticed into buying regular-priced goods too when attractive pieces are displayed.

A seconds sale will only work once or twice a year. Otherwise, the strategy loses its appeal through overexposure. Shops handling your normal goods will lose interest in selling your work if they must compete on a higher price scale. But once- or twice-a-year sales are usually considered okay. Some craftsmen recognize the economic advantage of selling seconds and relegate a number of their first-quality pieces for sale to improve the selection and keep customers returning. Under the guise of a seconds sale, you can offer regular merchandise at sale prices while avoiding the tag of price cutting.

Crafts less susceptible to quality-control problems or those where pieces can be repaired may still adopt the seconds sale merchandising strategy. Instead of seconds, offer discontinued items, a once-a-year clearance, or inventory reduction sales. Any of these excuses for a sale can be promoted through direct mail (see Chapter 10) and advertising. There's nothing like a bargain to attract buyers.

Two Incomes for Craftsmen

As a craftsman you should recognize that there are two incomes to be earned—craft production income and sales income. If you can function effectively as a craftsman and a salesman in your own retail store, you may earn both incomes. Only a few craftsmen are equipped with the right combination of mental skills and attitude to operate in both worlds effectively. Look at these examples—

In an art colony setting Mary Bonneville retains the craftswoman's one-of-a-kind design philosophy in her woven hangings, ponchos, rugs, and bags. She works diligently at her enormous loom located in a big picture window fronting on the main street that curves around the harbor. In addition to her own creations, Mary sells related items from other craftsmen. Mary buys directly from craftsmen, such as Paula Simmonds, at wholesale.

Paula Simmonds sells her knitted tams, socks, and other creations at the Bonneville Studio. She sells through a number of outlets all over the Puget Sound region because she prefers to produce and let others sell her goods. Paula raises her own sheep, shears the wool, and spins the yarn herself to fashion her knitted crafts. The sheep that Paula tends are selected for the color of their wool because she uses it naturally without dyes. Her sheep range in color from deep black through various shades of earthy browns to off-white.

Mary Bonneville does not take work in for sale on consignment, because she doesn't believe in consignment selling. "A silversmith may create a trayful of delightful rings, say, and leave them with a gallery on consignment. Since jewelry is kept in locked display cases and handled only by a sales person, it doesn't become shopworn. If it doesn't sell, the jeweler takes it back and displays it somewhere else. But a weaver can't do that," Mary states emphatically. "Every browser likes to feel the texture of one of my ponchos, and I would too, if I were considering buying it. After three or four months a poncho can look shopworn, even threadbare from constant fingering. If the gallery turns back a shopworn poncho left on consignment, what does the weaver have left? Nothing!"

Mary follows the line that crafts should be one-of-a-kind originals. Each warp she threads into her loom emerges as a unique product. Useful or functional weavings, such as ponchos, carpets, and bags, compete at prices potential buyers compare with similar articles available in stores—higher in price, but limited to unique designs. But wall hangings rich in texture, color, and design, become non-functional art pieces—and prices escalate to $300 to $1,500 depending on size, design, and materials. Ponchos may be priced at $90 to $150 in fluffy, luxuriant mohair.

Talking with customers interrupts her weaving, so mostly she lets browsers wander through the three showrooms converted from a house. From 10 A.M. to 5 P.M. six days a week, Mary busily fashions her exquisite weavings from her own designs employing fibers imported from more than fifty countries outside the United States.

"Summers and the period between Thanksgiving and Christmas

are the best times," she relates. Visitors attracted to the gallery shows and previews at other craft and art studios nearby spill into her showroom. Since most of her goods are priced out of the impulse dollar range, one or two sales a day generate considerable cash volume. "The town attracts traffic and my loom in the window brings them into the studio. Once there, the goods sell themselves, so I continue weaving until someone wants to buy." Hers is an unusual approach, but it works.

Mary converted two front rooms of a small house into her studio and sales gallery. She and her daughter live in the back. This arrangement reduces overhead costs. Further, when Mary's daughter is not in school, she helps customers find a poncho or wall hanging. The daughter's sales help relieves Mary from interrupting her weaving. Goods from other craftsmen augment her own production to increase sales volume to help cover her already low overhead. Lack of variety and only a few craft items for sale can become a problem if you try operating your own retail shop without selling other crafts.

Co-op Sales Outlets

Co-operatives, guilds, and associations offer another way craftsmen can participate in their own retail sales to gain a bigger piece of the retail price pie. Three different organizational forms for operating co-ops are currently in use in various parts of the United States. All co-ops benefit from a sharing of overhead expenses, greater variety and number of crafts offered for sale, and access to a larger potential buying public. By joining together in a co-op or association, craftsmen improve their income without losing control of the marketing function. The three forms of co-ops are:

❖ Communal retail outlet where craftsmen operate independently.

❖ Formal association where craftsmen form a corporation to act as a legal vehicle for their marketing operations.

❖ Association of individual shops and stalls that together draw traffic to a specific area. Each of these forms has its own problems and benefits.

The Craftsmen's Mall is an example of the communal retail outlet. It opened in a storefront along one of the busiest streets in downtown Miami. Five craftsmen banded together to share expenses and shop-minding time—the first benefit. Silver and gold jewelry, handcrafted leather, candles, pottery, macramé, and metal sculpture were offered in great variety—the second benefit. Shared space provides wall and floor displays of each craftsman's work plus a work bench for production on site. The fragrance of perking coffee mingles with the subtle scent of one or more candles and the pungent odor of burning flux from soldering during business hours.

In the communal co-op each of the craftsmen operates independently. Informally they share rent, utilities, and promotion expenses, such as printed handbills. When one craftsman is away, one of the others waits on customers for that person's crafts. Otherwise, each craftsman displays his own work, manages his own cash, keeps his own inventory, and files his own retail sales tax reports.

The Mall operates during the winter tourist season although not always in the same location. The group signs only a temporary lease to limit expenses. If the store should be rented to another tenant on a long-term lease, Craftsmen's Mall sets up shop in another location.

For a communal co-op to function effectively, each of the participating craftsmen must trust and understand the others. The participants need not be close friends, but they must respect the others' craftsmanship and integrity. Ordinarily, a leader will draw the others into the group and assume responsibility for finding and renting space. All help to decorate the premises, but each one arranges his own workspace and displays. The three to five or six craftsmen divvy up rent according to the space occupied with a bigger share paid by the craftsman located in one or more window locations. Other duties, such as designing handbills, sweeping, or helping with publicity, are shared. Since each craftsman manages his own cash and accounting, these business affairs are not commingled. The communal form of a co-op is not usually adaptable to a large group, as the informal understandings and sharing can become burdensome. For larger groups a more formal organization, such as a corporation, is needed (see Chapter 12). A number of publications detailing how to form a co-operative association along with sample legal papers are noted in Appendix.

A Show of Hands, the crafts co-op in New York City, has a membership of thirty-five to forty, according to the director. Considerable latitude on pricing is allowed to each craftsman whose work passes the scrutiny of the selection committee. In addition to a one-time joining fee of $50, each member pays $12 each month as a hanging fee. Sales efforts are shared by the members, as each must contribute eight hours of work each month to the shop's operation. Although some members live out of the New York City area, they pay someone to cover their eight-hour stint. Instead of simply minding the store and talking with customers, some members with special skills and interests handle accounting, displays, promotion, and general chores.

Financially the co-op aims to break even by retaining only 25 per cent of the sales price for pieces sold instead of the usual 33⅓ or 40 per cent kept by consignment shops. Expenses for A Show of Hands run fairly steep for their prime location. But crafts of professional quality sell, and the operation remains a co-operative effort. As in the communal form, a craftsman with a flair for organizing and merchandising is needed to take the risks of collecting the group, formalizing the organizational structure, locating space for a shop, and fiddling with the innumerable details of getting a store under way. Sharing the duties among several interested craftsmen can result in a co-op retail shop that promises greater success than any one craftsman attempting to operate alone. For the individual craftsman who wishes to do his own thing, sharing a group setting can solve the problem of attracting customers.

Hidden Harbor offers a different approach to co-op sharing. The owner converted a barnlike store into an enclosed mall with small, individual shops opening off the sheltered pedestrian space. Fourteen small shops occupy both sides of the mall. Crafts range from candles to block prints, jewelry, ceramics, macramé, and fabric prints, plus paintings. Although each shop operates independent of the others, the collection of shops and variety of crafts offered draw more visitors and potential buyers than would a single shop. Grouping of craft shops into a central location attracts buyers and shoppers for the same reason many shops cluster into shopping centers. Hidden Harbor permits an individual craftsman to rent space beginning at $75/month. Most of the craftsmen produce at a small work bench as part of their shop for two reasons—to authenticate the handwork displayed and to utilize every minute possible for increased production.

Craft Village attracts individual craftsmen to a central location with individual shops and studios in line around a center parking area. Retail shops vary in size and some offer materials, finished crafts, and instruction. But all of the shops are craft related and benefit from Village publicity and promotion.

Public Market Sales

A happy medium between street peddling (see Chapter 4) and your own retail shop is rented counter space in a public market. Sometimes called a Farmer's Market, these special places in many cities offer growers space to sell their produce directly to the public. With the decline in the number of growers, counter space often remains unused. To gain additional income and to broaden the slipping appeal of the public market, management rents stalls and counters to craftsmen for selling directly to patrons. Typical of the craftsmen and craftswomen profiting from these opportunities are Teppi and Peppi—T & P Handcrafts. Teppi and Peppi, two girls in their mid-twenties, rent eight feet of counter workspace. They offer a limited variety of inexpensive jewelry for sale to passersby. Their most popular products are handcrafted wire, bead, and bauble earrings that sell for $2 to $5 a pair. They also sell inexpensive cuff links, a few copper rings, and a wild variety of necklaces and chokers.

Teppi and Peppi are not really hippies, although their casual dress indicates little concern about appearances. While minding their counter-space store, they wear outlandish earrings—double the weight and several times the size that most women wear. Well aware of the need for attention-getting devices, the earrings become dangling, flashing displays. If a customer indicates an interest in earrings either of the girls is wearing, Teppi or Peppi will immediately slip the ear wires out of their pierced ears and offer the earrings for sale. If the earrings sell, she quickly slips on another sample. Although most of the earrings are fashioned with ear-wire findings, the girls will quickly exchange them for ear screws with a deft twist of their pliers.

Teppi and Peppi operate as T & P Handcrafts in Seattle's Pike

Place Market. While one may be talking at a mile-a-minute clip to a customer, the other will be hammering away at a necklace or choker design, shaping and assembling earrings, or hauling stock out of cardboard boxes piled behind their stools. A plastic display case with a stout lean-on top keeps small pieces out of reach of sticky fingers. A high board behind them displays far-out varieties of earrings and pendants plus many designs for conservative buyers. Earrings sell quickly on impulse to women who slip them on immediately and to men for gifts. Bead and bauble colors vary to suit every taste. Most of the earrings are fabricated from copper or stainless steel wire. The copper may be polished to a warm red or antiqued to a rich black.

Teppi and Peppi have proved that few limitations exist for earring designs—shape, size, weight, or color. "Some women will buy anything," Teppi reports. "They may not wear them, but they buy them and we never accept returns."

Teppi and Peppi rent space from the market at a nominal rate of $4 per day plus 5 per cent of their gross. They operate with a tax number and remit sales taxes monthly on their sales to the state. The market stays open six days a week, and either Teppi, Peppi, or both are on hand during peak shopping hours. Traffic through the market is heavy and constant, although summer and Christmas seasons attract more jewelry buyers. Out-of-towners find the market a quaint place to browse. Natives shop regularly for fresh produce, fish, and variety foods.

The girls net between $300–$500 a week, depending on season and weather. Summer months bring more tourists who spend more than natives. During the weeks between Thanksgiving and Christmas, sales peak at double the volume of ordinary weeks. After the first of the year, the two pack up and head out of town until spring.

T & P Handcrafts enjoys several pluses—low rent and a percentage of gross sales. Their investment is limited to portable display cases. Their high-traffic location exposes their crafts to a wide variety of customers with no promotion or advertising expense. Working on site helps maintain production, although they sometimes offer goods bought wholesale from others in their price range. The two girls limit sales to jewelry only, mostly of their own design and production. Their craft activities, hammering, working with pliers, and soldering with a torch in view of passersby, attract attention. Once a visitor stops to look and ponder, he or she will usually buy something.

Other craftsmen offering scented candles, handcrafted leather goods, wood carvings, artificial flowers, decorated driftwood, block printed note papers, and other crafts come and go along the handcrafts section of the market. Counter space rents by the day as craftsmen move in and set up shop. After lunch a market employee moves along the section and collects daily rent in cash. The show of craftsmen in action varies continually and shoppers like to browse. If they can examine crafts while shopping for food, they will frequently buy inexpensive items for gifts, bridge prizes, or for their own use. Further, the market is a happy location.

Operating Your Retail Shop

Don't dive blindly into establishing your own retail shop. Instead, consider the pluses and minuses in detail, preferably by writing out your plan—as described in Figure 5 later in this chapter. If possible, start small, conserve your capital, learn as you earn, and don't expect to turn a profit on your sales activity for several months—possibly for as long as a year—in a fixed location. As a guide, consider these proved success ideas in order—

SELECTING A NAME

What you call your shop can spark the curiosity of potential customers and catch the interest of writers, craft patrons, and contemporaries. It should be original, catchy, descriptive, and short. Leafing through "Guide to the Craft World," a sprinkling of eye-catching names for shops and galleries pops out—Iron Goose, The Spring Street Pottery, The Tannery, Sticks and Stones, The Clay People, Fibers, Ayottes' Designery, Artisan's Gallery, and Tatterdemalions Thingamajigs, to name a few. If you're stuck for a shop name, consider calling it a gallery.

People interested in art and creative pursuits think good thoughts when they hear the word "gallery." A few ideas for your gallery are:

❖ Tack on a descriptive word, such as Clay Gallery, Gallery of Needlecrafts, or the Red Barn Gallery.

❖ If your shop will be in or near a popular location, work that name into the title for your shop, such as Apple Lane Gallery, Waterfront Crafts Gallery, or Fountain Square Gallery.

❖ If your name is well established in your area through publicity, consider using your own name, as in Teddy's Gallery, Jane Arden's Gallery, or Crittenden's Craft Gallery.

Brainstorm for your shop's name, and challenge your creative associates to suggest possibilities. Jot all of them down on a big sheet of paper. When you have thirty or forty ideas, begin to weed them out one by one. Or combine a good word from one with a good idea from another. When you have the selection down to three or four, sketch a number of graphic ideas for each possibility—business stationery, a logo for a sign out front, and graphics for displays. The right combination of name and graphics seldom appears without creatively stalking numerous ideas. Beginning with the right name is important because your publicity and exposure build name familiarity. Make sure the familiarity builds on a sprightly, sales-oriented image.

SELECTING A LOCATION

Unless your gallery draws customers from traffic already in the vicinity, your shop must draw them on its own—a chancy proposition for a new shop and difficult even for an established shop. T & P Handcrafts at the public market sells to persons who come to the area for other shopping. Mary Bonneville attracts browsers from people drawn to the many shops and galleries in the arts and crafts colony. If your area already concentrates gift, antique, and crafts outlets into a special enclave, endeavor to join the crowd. You'll benefit from added traffic in the same way car buyers move from showroom to showroom along every city's auto row. Other ideas to consider when selecting a location are:

❖ Look for parking nearby. Craft buyers will likely come by car. If your shop is also on a bus line, great, but parking is more important.

❖ Personal security ranks high when choosing a location if you plan to offer lessons at night. Muggers and purse snatchers in an area discourage visitors from attending previews at night or holiday shoppers during pre-Christmas evening hours.

❖ Pick only the size shop you can afford and use. A space that is too small may eliminate production equipment. A space that is too large could be costly and expensive to decorate.

❖ Hold out for a street-level entrance. Asking browsers or casual visitors to hike upstairs or wait for elevators can cut shop traffic to a half or a third. Settle for other than street-level space only if other craft or art spaces are clustered on an upper floor or on all floors of a building. Visitors will move off the street if several galleries offer browsing interest.

DECORATING FOR LOW COST

Before signing a lease, sketch a few ideas for front entry decoration and interior refurbishment of the shop space. Most low-cost spaces call for considerable upgrading and refurbishment. Substitute your creative talent for cash to create an atmosphere that uniquely projects your shop's image and style. An attractive and promotable refurbishing need not cost a bundle of your already short cash if you look into these possibilities:

❖ Antiques and crafts complement each other, so dress up rusty iron grillwork, an old wagon, an antique loom, or farm equipment to fit your entry or to display craft selections in a window. Antique or just plain old and discarded pieces draw attention when painted in bright colors and combined with fabrics, driftwood, and needlework crafts.

❖ Supergraphics can set a storefront apart from the rest of the street with a creative design and a few cans of paint. Upgrading existing surfaces without much physical change but with paint or fabric can make startling changes.

❖ Carry through the antique theme inside by displaying crafts on refurbished desks, tables, and display cases long since discarded by others.

❖ Install perforated hardboard on the walls for a double benefit— low cost and a flexible surface for displaying all types of crafts from wall hangings to pottery.

❖ Plan to use as much of the original shop as possible. Even if an old wood floor appears impossible, rent a sander and remove the surface rather than attempt to cover it with carpeting or tile. Install peel-and-stick tiles on a concrete floor yourself; it's easy and provides a colorful working floor. Paint a high ceiling black and install a net or wood grill rather than build in an all-new ceiling.

❖ Show your crafts in use. Innovative racks for hanging earrings, place settings on a dining table to show pottery in use, candles in gift wrappings—all suggest ideas for using your crafts. Don't depend on your customer's imagination to find a use for your crafts. When Teppi and Peppi wear eye-popping earrings, necklaces, and bracelets, they actively display their wares—and change in a moment if a customer buys a pair of earrings they happen to be wearing. Earrings and jewelry look best when hanging naturally. Rings can be slipped onto stubs of limbs cut from a bush and flocked or sprayed. A choker or necklace may hang from a simulated neckline cut from cardboard or fabricated from papier-mâché. Brainstorm ideas for creative display of your crafts just as intensely as you create new designs. Candle shops featuring unusual creations attract attention with burning candles through sight and scent. The flickering flames attract browsers to the glow-wax designs or fascinating wax carvings in the shape of birds and small animals. Although these exotic candles may actually be lighted, they include short wicks to limit burning to a cavity large enough for a replaceable votive. Attractions like the flickering candles need not be expensive and they cue sales.

Conserve your available cash by trading off elbow grease and creative ideas for expensive redecoration. Getting started is guaranteed to cost more than you thought possible. Decorating is one place you can keep costs down by displaying your creative artistry.

PLANNING FOR SECURITY

Shoplifting continues to be a problem for every store from supermarket to gallery. When a shoplifter walks off with one of your creations or a craft in your shop on consignment, you lose it all. One help is to design displays to minimize shoplifting. You can't keep everything behind bars or glass because shoppers like to pick up and examine crafts before buying. A few of the ideas successful shop owners use to maintain security are:

❖ Keep small crafts under complete control while maintaining visibility. Jewelry is so small and easy to palm or slip into a pocket that it should be displayed only under a glass cover with locked access. Shoppers can pore over jewelry without slipping a ring over a finger or trying on earrings. Leave about a third of the price tags with the prices showing; turn down the others to pique curiosity. When a customer asks to see a specific piece, hand it to her and stick with her until she either returns the piece to you or buys it. Always return each piece under the glass before showing another.

❖ Small pots or ceramic pieces can be displayed on shelves behind a counter in full view. When a customer asks to see one close, hand it to him: Wall hangings can usually be displayed where customers can examine them up close as they are too big to hide.

❖ Big pots or metal sculptures can be left in the open as their size prevents them from being taken.

❖ Arrange displays of candles, wood toys, and similar crafts on individual blocks or spaces. When one is sold, replace it with another immediately. That way you can see at a glance if anything is missing.

❖ Keep your most valuable pieces together, preferably near your work bench or at the back of the shop. Concentrate your attention on those pieces when customers are in the shop. You can't watch all of your valuable pieces if they are scattered.

❖ Arrange note papers and other small but inexpensive items in wire racks hung from perforated hardboard walls. With only one package in a rack, you can see when one is missing. Replace sold items immediately if you have a back stock or remove the rack to avoid empties.

When customers are browsing in your shop, maintain surveillance without being obvious. Don't continue working at your bench unless your crafts are too big to handle easily. Train clerks to watch for shoplifters but encourage them to allow customers to handle and examine your crafts closely.

When you combine a retail shop with a teaching facility, you must, of course, include extra space. One exception to the advice about minimum space is a working area that attracts attention. At the Bonneville Weaving Studio, Mary works at her enormous loom in front of a big picture window facing the sidewalk and street. The loom stops traffic and turns passersby into browsers and, hopefully, buyers.

A work bench where you can busily work at your craft never ceases to attract attention. At the Craftsmen's Mall, Mike Dodd hammers and works with pliers and propane torch in handcrafting sterling silver jewelry at his prime location in the storefront window. People are attracted by action. Mike's activities in the craft shop fascinate strollers or shoppers and entice them into the shop. Working at a bench serves another purpose—it makes extra productive hours available when the shop is open but no customers are present.

BUILDING A VARIETY

Plan a suitable mix for inventory—enough to attract customers but not so much that your turnover is low and inventory investment high. Many craft sales outlets aim for a minimum inventory turnover six times a year. That means annual sales represent six times the average value of inventory. Fast moving lines may turn over every month, possibly more often. Less interesting goods may lie on the shelf for a full year. Good retailing practice calls for moving out those goods that won't sell by offering special prices or conducting close-out sales. A Wall Street maxim, "Cut your losses short," applies here. A craftsman dislikes slashing prices on his own designs, but a retailer understands the need for inventory turnover if the shop is to profit.

Sell related crafts from other producers. How many related crafts should be stocked? Choices range from the individual shops where only a single craftsman's works are sold to large stores that sell the work of as many as two thousand producing craftsmen. As a single craftsman, limit the number of lines you handle at first to reduce bookkeeping and space requirements. But, even if you plan to sell your own work primarily, select complementary products in other media. You build sales volume by appealing to more browsers. To minimize your investment initially, accept crafts only on consignment. As your retail business develops and you gain confidence, switch to buying crafts from other craftsmen at wholesale to earn a 50 per cent markup rather than the usual third for consignments. Your own interests, space limitations, location, and clerical time available will determine how many other craftsmen's products you can handle.

Plan to offer craft supplies, tools, findings, and equipment in a separate section of your store for at least three reasons: (1) When you buy materials in larger quantities, you reduce your own costs. As a retailer of materials, tools, and equipment, you qualify for a wholesaler's discount. (2) Sales of craft supplies can generate considerable dollar volume and contribute toward paying overhead—rent, utilities, business licenses, accounting, and all the other expenses of being in business. (3) Other craftsmen bring visitors with them when they stop to purchase supplies. Or they will refer friends to your shop. Don't go overboard in stocking many pieces of expensive equipment. Instead, stock materials that are most often used along with hand tools and popular but inexpensive equipment. Take orders for expensive equipment from a catalogue to reduce your investment in inventory while offering a full selection.

Supply other shops with your craft products by mail. Or sell directly to individuals by mail from the stock in your shop. See Chapter 7 for ideas on marketing by mail. Increasing the turnover of your own craft pieces builds profits with little increase in overhead. Filling mail orders can occupy a clerk's time when shop traffic is light. Or you can hire a part-timer to fill orders at odd times —evenings or weekends to gain full utilization from your shop space.

PROMOTING YOUR GALLERY

Promote your shop through as many channels as time and money permit. Advertise selectively, if at all. Instead, depend on publicity and promotion through shows and demonstrations. Chapter 2 details a variety of low-cost, effective promotion ideas to bring buyers into your shop. Promotion is the name of the game for the successful shop owner even when yours is in a high traffic area. The more people who know about your shop, the more traffic you can expect. You play the percentage game with traffic. Some will buy, so the more traffic, the more sales.

GETTING STARTED

If at all possible, gain some in-shop experience by working in a successful shop or gallery. Then pick the brains of the owner in exchange for your time. Ask about rents, promotion ideas, accounting, taxes, sales strategy, turnover ratios, and selection of goods for sale. There is really no substitute for on-site experience before you take the plunge in opening your own shop.

Plan your shop on paper before spending your first dime. Detail all of the elements in a single expense and sales plan to see if your ideas can turn a profit as in Fig. 5. Note the important elements of sales volume and expense. Even when you estimate or forecast sales and expenses, a detailed, intelligent guess at the pieces will help you gain an over-all picture. Look at these specific items:

❖ Sales volume will always be a guess before you open the shop. Forecast sales by an expected daily volume according to experience from others. A low and hopeful forecast will show how volume affects the "bottom line"—the profit payoff all businesses aim for.

❖ Cost of goods sold becomes an important element of operating profit. Consider your gallery as a separate operation—its own cost center in financial terms. Price your own goods at wholesale when determining cost of goods sold. Goods acquired from other craftsmen for sale can be priced at two-thirds retail or 60 per cent, depending on your ability to attract complementary crafts with a high payout. See Chapter 3 for pricing philosophy. In the example detailed in Fig. 5, two thirds of the gross sales are of the owner's products with a gross commission of 50 per cent; one third are consignment sales with a gross commission of 33⅓ per cent.

❖ Operating profit is a subtotal of gross sales less cost of goods sold. Subtracting overhead and other expenses from the operating profit yields a bottom line net profit.

❖ Overhead expenses should be estimated closely, as they are critical. Include a monthly share of nonrecurring start-up expenses spread over your lease period. For a one-year lease with an option for another year, plan to write off shop refurbishment, business license, legal fees, and other one-time costs over the first year. The $100 charge for start-up represents a monthly amortization of $1,200 nonrecurring costs. Recognize that overhead expenses remain essentially the same regardless of sales volume.

❖ Administrative and selling expenses may vary somewhat according to sales volume. For low sales volume, you could handle customers without a clerk. When volume increases, you would be money ahead to hire a full- or part-time clerk to conserve your bench time for producing crafts. But don't forget to include an allowance for some of your time at every volume of sales. Unless you charge selling time for yourself when talking with customers, you work for nothing. A detailed plan will help you determine whether you gain more income by producing crafts and selling them in your own shop or selling your production to others at wholesale or on consignment.

❖ Profit or loss results from gallery operation only, as you have al-

Fig. 5: Gemstone Gallery

Monthly Profit Plan

	Low	Hopeful
Sales	$1,500	$3,600
Cost of Goods Sold		
Bench products @ 50%	500	1,200
Consignments @ 66 2/3%	333	800
Operating Profit	$667	$1,600
Overhead Expenses		
Shop rent	180	180
Maintenance	60	60
Utilities	22	22
Insurance	25	25
Taxes	10	10
Start-up amortization	100	100
	$397	$397
Administrative & Selling Expenses		
Clerk		400
Selling time	200	100
Promotion	30	60
Bookkeeping	40	50
Miscellaneous expense & contingency	40	50
	$310	$600
Profit (Loss)	($40)	$543

ready earned a producer's profit on the goods sold. Whether the bottom line profit compensates for the risks, only you can decide. You can see how sensitive profits are to sales volume. All of the factors noted earlier—location, traffic, pricing, and promotion—affect sales volume. As a gallery manager, you must determine the mix that optimizes profits. Unless you can juggle the important factors to gain a satisfactory sales volume, you might do better to stick with producing and let marketing specialists sell your goods. By operating your own shop, you may be selling more of your production than if you depend on others.

Chapter 7

SELLING YOUR CRAFTS AND
KNOW-HOW BY MAIL

Money in your mailbox! Selling by mail attracts individual craftsmen as well as importers. Mail-order sellers from India, Hong Kong, Europe, and nearly every other country in the world compete directly in the world-wide market available to you through the U. S. Post Office. Selling by mail introduces a new and exciting dimension for making money from your crafts. Look at these reasons behind exploding mail-order craft businesses:

Interest in crafts and the cash people are willing to spend on crafts are expanding rapidly with the result that the volume of business available through the mail is exploding. Rockhounds no longer satisfied with picking up and polishing local agates can buy fire opals directly from Australia. Jewelry craftsmen can buy findings and odd materials from a two hundred-page color-filled catalogue issued three times a year. Because craftsmen are so specialized and their interests so diverse, they constitute a "thin" market. A store selling jewelry findings and sterling materials might struggle along on local sales only, but it can expand its market one hundred-fold through the mail. While the total market for crafts is expanding, elements of it are splintering. You can reach these diverse specialties effectively only through the mail.

Craftsmen interested in materials and many buyers of gift merchandise prefer to shop from a catalogue rather than hoof it to shops or shows. Catalogues describe selections of materials and equipment more precisely than personal inspection from a limited stock.

Mail-order markets for crafts offer better opportunities for selling materials, training, and equipment than for finished products. People buy things and services by mail even when they can't see and touch them in person. Since many crafts depend on eye appeal and buyer impulse to sell, mail-order offers fewer chances for selling rings, macramé belts, and candles to individual buyers than a shop. But craft materials, tools, and know-how will sell to other craftsmen through the mail. Items that sell directly to the beginner or inexperienced craftsmen are the do-it-yourself (DIY) kits requiring minimum skills to complete, such as macramé kits complete with materials, designs, and detailed instructions, stitchery designs printed on backing with hanks of yarn for completing a specific project according to detailed instructions, and yarn kits with knitting wool and instructions for a specific project. Many other DIY kits and materials move directly into the hands of the beginning or amateur craftsman where instruction constitutes a large part of the product. Finished craft products can be sold by mail, but you must offer something unique. Further, you must compete with local craftsmen on price and delivery to be successful. More details on that later in this chapter.

With the whole world to sell to, how do you market by mail?

❖ First, you must catch a buyer's attention through advertising, shows, or reputation.

❖ Second, you must convince a prospect that he should buy your product either as a new item or in place of something else he may be considering.

❖ Third, you must motivate the buyer to write a check, fill in an order blank, stuff the lot in an envelope, and then wait two, three, or four weeks for his order to arrive in the mail.

A tough assignment? You bet!

People buy by mail when they can't find what they want locally at a price they can afford to pay. For most goods sold by mail, price will usually be less important than availability. Uniqueness and the thin market concept apply about equally in mail-order selling. A jewelry craftsman producing sterling rings on a San Juan island in Washington State may offer designs similar to those available from a producing jeweler in New York City. He would find it difficult to sell finished rings by mail to New York customers. But a supplier of special waxes for developing models could sell to jewelry craftsmen all over the world—and does.

Developing a mail-order market for your finished products, materials, or tools requires patience. Don't attempt to force a rapid expansion of a mail-order business. Start small and build as you learn. Patience allows you to profit from your mistakes before they overwhelm you.

Few absolute answers exist for questions on effective mail-order selling. Each craft develops its own peculiarities. Learn what you can from those who are already successful, but don't be afraid to experiment or innovate when developing your own business. Selling crafts or craft know-how by mail requires more of a business-oriented approach than any other facet of craft marketing.

Selling Craft Products by Mail

Selling on Consignment—Gift shops and consignment sale outlets accept craft products submitted by mail. Properly approached, these shops offer a continuing outlet for volume production rather than one-at-a-time sales directly to retail buyers. You stand a better chance of selling if you contact shop buyers initially through a show or in person. But you can still sell craft products by mail. For example—

Studio 714 sells directly to gift shops in nearly every state west of the Mississippi. Bill Garrison sells at wholesale prices rather than on consignment. Wholesale prices, as has been noted, are set at 50 per cent off the expected selling price. Selling wholesale minimizes two common problems in selling by mail—record keeping and credit problems. Keeping track of which pieces on consignment have sold, been paid for, returned, or still out can absorb an inordinate number of hours that might be better spent on craft production. Selling wholesale also generates immediate cash (within the normal 30–60-day billing cycle). These advantages offset the lower net return from the 50 per cent markup.

New customers may be contacted through a variety of leads— Chamber of Commerce listings of gift shops, brochures issued by tourist organizations, notices in various craft magazines, and word of mouth. Acquiring new accounts calls for continuing activity. The Garrisons send a representative group of Garrison Originals to a potential outlet as a sample kit. Included with the shipment is a catalogue of all jewelry items they are prepared to supply along with terms of purchase. To assure arrival, he insures each shipment and requests a return receipt. He also includes a prepaid mailer for returning the sample pieces. In all of his shipments to date, only one potential outlet has failed to return his samples. While he risks the loss of his representative pieces, he understands that few shop owners order and pay for goods sight unseen. Actually sending sample kits focuses a potential customer's attention immediately on hard goods where a colorful brochure may be swiftly discarded. Shipping samples short-cuts the selling cycle by one full step. Instead of asking a shop owner to request samples, then ship the samples, and wait for an order, the shop owner can decide immediately whether Garrison Originals will sell in his shop. Bill asks only for a small order at first —again to reduce his risks. Gift shops are not always the best credit risks. Selling by mail may entail a few bad accounts unless the poor and slow payers are eliminated at the beginning. Further, he never ships a second order until the first is paid.

Studio 714 markets a range of low- to medium-price jewelry. The Garrisons can afford to risk a sample set of their low-cost items— usually half a dozen of their most popular quick movers. At their cost, sample sets run less than $10—enough to command consideration when they arrive, yet not a great loss if the pieces should not be returned. The shop may keep the samples and pay the invoice enclosed or return the sample set. Since a return package with postage is furnished, the shop owner can return the sample with minimum effort. This act psychologically eliminates any feeling of obligation. Sample sets are frequently returned with an order for more expensive items. Along with the first order, Bill requires a deposit of 20 per cent of the order value in cash to assure genuine interest. The remainder is invoiced along with the shipment.

Using this system, Studio 714 acquires a new customer on an average of one in ten at a cost of shipping the sample set both directions. Careful culling of prospects has improved the ratio of initial sales from one in twenty when they started. Prospects who order have been unusually good about reordering, usually in larger and larger quantities because Garrison Originals offer excellent handcrafted quality in a price range that sells on impulse to shop browsers. As the name implies, Garrison Originals are one-of-a-kind pieces, although some similarity exists among the various lines. Fast-moving items include metalcrafted dangling earrings priced for sale at $2 to $5. Much of the Studio 714 line is produced in silver both with and without gemstones. Metalcrafted and cast pieces are included in their popular lines. To sustain orders, Studio 714 regularly sends catalogue information to their shops announcing new items, revised prices, and discontinued items.

One key element in the Studio 714 plan is an iron-clad replacement guarantee. If items fail to sell in a shop within a reasonable period, the owner may return slow-moving goods for full credit on a new shipment—but not for a cash refund. Offering to trade merchandise eliminates a shop owner's concern about inventorying goods that might not sell. Items that don't sell in one locality often sell quickly in another. Sometimes, an item will not sell in any outlet—so, that item is discontinued. Returned merchandise can usually be sold at a reduced price at one of the summer fairs attended by the Garrisons.

While the Garrisons sell on a wholesale basis and simplify their record keeping, a number of shops will accept craft goods only on consignment. Women's association shops, for lack of a better all-inclusive term, sell only on consignment. In addition to the woman's exchanges which operate mainly in eastern states, consignment shops may be operated by guilds, leagues, or associations functioning as fund-raising auxiliaries of hospital, church, or special-interest groups. Often these consignment shops are staffed by volunteers, and members of the various groups form a sizable clientele because of the publicity afforded the shops through organization newsletters and announcements.

A typical woman's exchange consignment shop is The Country Store operated by the Junior Service League of Chapel Hill, North Carolina. In addition to the articles for sale from local craftsmen, The Country Store accepts craft goods on consignment from distant craftsmen by mail. The store displays and sells the work of more than two hundred craftsmen and exhibits a surprising variety of crafts. Here is how you, as an individual-producing craftsman, would go about selling to consignment shops similar to The Country Store.

Write to the shop for a copy of the general rules and specifications for marking and pricing. Updated lists of shops that sell on consignment are catalogued in "Guide to the Craft World" (see Appendix under *Artisan Crafts* for address). Or keep an eye out for shops in one or more of the craft magazines. Before you can be accepted as a consignor, you will be asked to submit a sample of your craftwork for inspection and screening. Your work will be judged by a committee and the paid manager, if the shop supports one. Acceptance of your work depends on the media, type of article, quality of workmanship and materials, and the selling price. If your work passes the screening, you will usually be assigned a number that identifies you as an accepted consignor.

Check the shop's commission rate. The Country Store keeps 30 per cent of the retail selling price to support its local schools, library, day-care center, YW-YMCA, and other designated charities. In addition, you may be charged a once-a-year fee to cover part of the expenses of correspondence, bookkeeping, display, and advertising. At The Country Store the annual fee amounts to only one dollar: Shipments to the store are prepaid and any goods will be returned at your expense. You will be asked to sign a "hold harmless" agreement that any fire, theft, or accidental damage losses to your craftwork will be at your expense. Although most shops buy insurance against losses, the hold-harmless agreements protect them against lawsuits. If your crafts are subject to breakage, the hold-harmless agreement covers potential accidents too.

When sending crafts for sale to a consignment shop, you must follow that shop's rules about labeling—retail price, name and address, and consignor number. Most shops take inventory twice a year and send you a list of your goods still in inventory according to the shop's records. When you receive your inventory, check it against your own records. If you note any discrepancies, write to the shop for clarification immediately.

Some consignment shops solicit special orders from customers. On custom pieces, you will be asked to quote prices before beginning any project and to satisfy any reasonable complaints when the piece is inspected by the customer.

Retailing Directly to Mail-Order Customers—Selling craft products directly to consumers involves a two-step contact. First, you kindle enough interest by the customer to request a catalogue or folder which describes numerous and varied crafts. Second, the folder must generate enough interest for the prospect to order and send money. Selling a prospect directly through an advertisement seldom pays because the cost of picturing a variety of craft products becomes excessively expensive. The economics of selling directly to the consumer calls for a relatively high markup. Most mail-order marketers figure they must sell a product for five times its unburdened cost; that is, the cost of the product without allowances for overhead or selling expenses. A ring that costs $2.50 in material and production time should sell for $12.50 to generate enough money to pay for overhead and selling expenses.

Note these other factors about selling direct to consumers by mail: Marketing costs include not only the advertising or publicity but the cost of producing the salable products, mailing, and handling orders. Publicity can substitute for some advertising. Direct mail, where you send folders or catalogues to a select list of prospects, can short-cut the two-step system. But direct mail can be expensive unless you can find an active list—preferably a list of previous buyers of jewelry, hand-screened note pads, batik scarves, or whatever craft you are producing. Postage and insurance will cost little for mailing most small jewelry pieces, but shipping could be prohibitively expensive for pottery. All of these factors must be weighed carefully in a thoroughly planned program before embarking on a sell-by-mail campaign.

Selling catalogue craft items by mail presupposes a production capacity for multiple copies of the same or very similar items. A ring with an onyx gemstone set in a sterling mount pictured in a brochure or catalogue should be available in quantity, perhaps several hundred copies. Craftsmen who prefer to create one-of-a-kind designs rather than produce multiple copies of one quantity-selling item should avoid mail-order selling direct to consumers.

Direct mail-order selling requires considerable capital. First, you must produce an attractive brochure or catalogue. Examine some of the "junk mail" that arrives in your mailbox. Most of the pieces include considerable color printing and graphically pleasing arrays of photographs illustrating the products offered for sale. Brochures include two costs—art and type composition ready for printing and the printing itself. The copy preparation will cost the same whether you plan to print 100 copies or 100,000. Printing costs vary according to the number of copies, as the plate and make-ready costs must be amortized over the run. Unless copy preparation and printing are well done, your sales literature could look hopelessly amateurish—a fault that will turn off all but the small minority of buyers who appreciate quaintness. Unless you are a qualified graphic designer and shoot photographs with professional quality, you will need artistic help and possibly an experienced writer to put together an effective brochure. Printing should be on good quality paper stock that reproduces as much of the quality in your photographs as possible. All of these elements cost money—most of it in cash or short-term credit. Even short-term credit will fall due before cash begins to flow from mail-order sales.

Time lag between the appearance of an ad or publicity and resulting sales means a lag between your investment and potential income. Some advertisements must be placed two or more months ahead of a magazine's publication date. Direct mail affords a much quicker response, but the added cost of "buying customers" by direct mail should be balanced against the time lag between investment and income.

Brochures, advertising, and the labor for physically handling orders from receipt of inquiries to shipment of finished pieces make up substantial selling expenses. Before embarking on a mail-order campaign, develop a plan that realistically accounts for these expenses and compare these costs with the markup kept by wholesale or consignment shops. Suppose you sell $24,000 retail value of your craft products in one year. If you sold your production at wholesale, you could reasonably expect to receive $12,000. Whether you can profit from sales at that figure depends on your pricing schedule and your efficiency in craft production. If you sold through consignment shops, you could reasonably expect to receive $16,000, figuring on a one-third retail commission. You must determine whether direct selling to consumers through the mail will sell $24,000 worth of craft products and net you $12,000 or $16,000. If mail-order selling can turn over $24,000 or more in gross volume and yield more spendable cash after paying for selling expenses, then you are ahead of the game.

Let's look at some of the prices. You can advertise for inquiries through classified-ad sections in craft magazines for $5 to $25 per in-

Fig. 6: Mail-Order Sales Campaign

Sales Objectives — Alt. 1 $10,000 Gross
                    — Alt. 2 $30,000 Gross

MARKETING PLAN

	Alt. #1	Alt. #2
Advertising—small displays plus classifieds	$ 4,000	$ 4,000
Brochures, one color — 1,000	500	500
— 20,000 direct mail		2,000
List expense		400
Order blanks and return envelopes	80	120
Postage on brochures	140	2,361
Postage & insurance on shipments (avg. $1.20)	600	1,800
Shipping supplies	100	300
Labor—filling and mailing orders	500	1,500
Total Marketing Expense	$ 5,920	$12,981
Sales — 500 (50% of brochure mailings in response to ads) at average sales of $20 (500 orders)	$10,000	
— 50% of brochure mailings (500 orders), 5% of direct mail (1,000 orders) average sale $20		$30,000
Marketing Expense (per cent of sales)	59.2%	43.3%
Operating Profit	$ 4,080	$17,019
Net Profit (Loss)	($920)	$2,019

Before embarking on a direct sales campaign, develop a profit plan that accounts for the above elements as a minimum. This sample campaign examines two alternatives. Alternative No. 1 uses advertising only and spends $4,000 to acquire leads. In response to the advertising, 1,000 brochures are mailed out and half of those receiving brochures order crafts averaging $20 per order. Thus, 500 orders at $20 average results in gross sales of $10,000. However, advertising plus printing and mailing cost $5,920 or 59.2 per cent of gross sales. If you figure you must get at least 50 per cent of the sales price for sales at the wholesale level, the operating profit of $4,080 shows a net loss of $920 for Alternative No. 1.

Alternative No. 2 combines the same advertising noted for Alternative No. 1 plus a direct mailing of 20,000 brochures to names purchased from a list broker. Sales are noted at 500 from brochures sent in response to ads plus 1000 or 5% of those receiving brochures by direct mail with an average amount of $20 each. Gross sales volume from both sources totals $30,000 at a cost of $12,981, which leaves an operating profit of $17,019. On the same basis of 50 per cent for wholesale price, Alternative No. 2 yields a net profit of $2,019 from marketing only.

sertion per month, depending on the number of words and the periodical's circulation. The classic text on how to write effective classified ads is a booklet, *Profits*, published by *Popular Mechanics*. For your copy send $1.00 to *Popular Mechanics*, 224 West 57th Street, New York, N.Y. 10019. A display ad will be more expensive with small ads costing $50 to $100 on up to $2,000–$10,000 or more for half or full pages in color. Most periodicals print their costs for classified ads at the beginning of the section. You must write to the advertising department for costs of display space. An advertising agency will help you prepare display ads and charge only for the copy preparation, that is, the cost of photographs, graphic layout, type composition, and final art preparation. The ad agency earns a 15 per cent discount from periodicals that covers most of the cost for creative help and co-ordination.

Brochures in one color may cost $.20 each for a single-page folder printed on two sides to $.50–$.60 each for a two-color eight-page brochure with a five thousand print order. Price per copy depends heavily on how many are printed at one time, as noted earlier. A plan for a mail-order selling campaign might look like the example in Fig. 6 in its basic elements. Unless you look at the costs and potential returns in total, you could be unpleasantly surprised by losing a bundle of your capital on an ill-advised mail-order venture.

Mail-order selling represents an iffy proposition at best. Start small by advertising or promoting your sales locally. Insist on complete originality when designing and producing your crafts, but learn to adapt your advertising and promotion from the best of what is already working for successful mail-order sellers. You can bet they learned what works and what doesn't work the hard, expensive way. Offer a limited selection of your products at first to minimize the cost of producing a sales brochure. As you find out what sells, expand your operation slowly. Build and expand on those elements that prove successful. Discard ruthlessly any part of your program that fails to generate sales. See Appendix for "Sources of Mailing Lists."

Frankly, many craftsmen do not have the patience and the head for business needed to pursue a mail-order craft business direct to the consumer. If you are a sensitive, creative craftsman, your mind may not be tuned to the hard-line methods and discipline needed to sell your products by mail.

Philip Morton, founder and prime mover of The Working Hand Craft Center of Bowling Green, Ohio, sold products from his shop profitably by mail before switching over to wholesale, using an agent. Phil Morton taught all types of jewelry metalcrafting at the University of Minnesota before setting up his teaching-producing craft center. He sells a striking line of contemporary jewelry from his own shop. He formerly sold to eleven other outlets by mail before deciding to let his agent handle the selling chores.

"I feel the most important element in a selling program is finding the right market," he says. "It doesn't matter how well crafts are designed and fabricated, they are dead in the wrong market. The typical gift store offers little or no market for my contemporary designs. Their customers are looking for antiques, period designs—or just plain junk.

"The second consideration is price. You must look for designs which can be produced profitably within the context of a competitive market because other good craftsmen are also at work."

Phil finds his outlets two ways—by personal contacts while traveling and by telephone. "Two ladies from Washington, D.C., were in our shop on Conneaut Avenue in Bowling Green. I overheard one of them say, 'This is very much like ——— shop in Bethesda, Maryland.' Later I asked them about the shop they referred to and jotted down the address. The ladies told me the shop carried a line of contemporary gifts. After they left, I telephoned the shop—less expensive than traveling. The shop owner indicated an interest, so I sent them samples on approval. Their first order totaled close to $1,000, and they have become one of my most productive outlets."

Talking with shop owners in person or by phone allows Phil to probe for customer interests and any specialties represented. One of the shops he supplies by mail sells only items related to owls, including many ceramics. To capture this market, he designed pendants and earrings in the shape of owls. "The owner was delighted to find a craftsman willing to cater to her very special product line—and you must admit, selling only owls limits a market."

Rings, particularly wedding rings, represent a major chunk of Phil Morton's volume. Selling wedding bands with and without stones at his Craft Center shop permits custom designing and fitting. Selling wedding bands by mail through shops poses other problems—mainly determining ring size. He solves this by selling six samples of rings to dealers who use the designs to solicit orders. Other design possibilities are offered from a sheet of drawings. A dealer taking an order carefully measures the ring size and notes the design desired. Phil crafts the ring to size and ships the custom-finished wedding ring back to the dealer by airmail, insured—faster than many local jewelers could construct a similar custom ring. Customers are delighted with the fast, custom service. Phil Morton voices impatience with ideas about "craftsmen not being businessmen."

"I believe that the craftsman, to be successful, must not only sell high-standard crafts, but he must also sell service and reliability," he says. "The one thing a retail shop *must* have is a *reliable* source. On-time deliveries to a shop build and preserve good customer relations and go along with quality in design and craftsmanship."

Costs are closely controlled at The Working Hand Craft Center. The key element is a job card for each piece or group of pieces produced. Since cost control affects pricing, his cost accounting system keeps the shop on a business basis.

Producing craftsmen run into the roadblock of time at some point in their career. "After all, a craftsman can produce only so many pieces with his own two hands," Phil Morton relates. "Sure, I can devise shortcuts and use special equipment to cut the bench time for each piece. But there is no way I can extend the number of hours in a day. Design becomes a major factor, and I design for simplicity and producibility as well as for visual and aesthetic effect. If you're not conscious of design as a limit on production, you can design yourself into a corner because time relates directly to cost and eventual pricing."

Phil Morton sells few of his crafts to individuals at retail. Previous customers will sometimes order directly by mail and buy additional pieces from simple drawings. He now uses an agent who concentrates his marketing on finding "the right outlet" for Phil's contemporary jewelry designs. Outlets that are right for him would not be right for selling stuffed animals and many other crafts. An agent can analyze the market and find those outlets that fit—otherwise, crafts will not sell. Then no one, the craftsman, agent, or outlet benefits.

Kit Sales—Alternative to Finished Product Sales

Craft materials packaged in a kit along with instructions have boomed with the growing interest in crafts. Major magazines, such as *Woman's Day, American Home, Ladies' Home Journal,* and others have featured stitchery kits, clock kits, materials and instructions for macramé, plastic parts for big jewelry, and many, many more. Methods for marketing kits through the mail can be as varied as the kits themselves.

Gemex sells directly to consumers through a mammoth two hundred-page catalogue that may include as many as seventy-two pages in full color. Producing a catalogue of this size three times a year represents a mammoth task and an expensive commitment. Of course, the catalogue contains many other elements than kits to make jewelry, but it is offered free for the asking. But you're not likely to get another unless the first catalogue produces an order. All mail-order operators from giant Sears, Roebuck on down keep detailed records of each customer's orders. Only those customers who order regularly and generate a minimum dollar volume continue to receive catalogues. Gemex also sells gems, lapidary equipment, materials, and tools in great variety. A supplier does not reach such volume overnight. Patience is an important element in the mail-order business.

If you are interested in developing a craft kit program for sale through the mail, begin locally first. You may sell kits from your own retail shop, on consignment, in connection with your teaching, or from a booth or bench at a local crafts fair. All of these opportunities for direct selling are detailed in other chapters.

The best place to begin a kit program is in connection with classes you teach in how to put the kits together. Hold classes in your home, studio, school system, or as a guest speaker at clubs. As you demonstrate how to use the materials and the variety of projects to be completed, refer frequently to the kit. It should include everything needed except such staples as pans or a bench to work on. Projects that can be marketed to housewives should require only a modicum of skill and a minimum of equipment. Plastic and paper flowercraft, weedcraft, and stick-together jewelry provide instant gratification for participants, and the needed skills can be learned in an afternoon.

Instructions packaged with kits mean the difference between a dissatisfied customer who may not finish even one project and a continuing succession of reorders. For example, each individually different stitch required to complete a stitchery design should be detailed in a step-by-step drawing. If you examine one of the kits sold through one of the major magazines, you will see how detailed are their instructions. One reason home sewing has become so popular is that complete instructions are packaged with each pattern.

Two kinds of instructions are necessary for a home-craft kit, such as a weedcraft or plastic-dip flowercraft kit. First, you should include a detailed step-by-step series of photographs to lead the neophyte pictorially by the hand through each of the steps. If you are not a photographer, barter some of your craftwork to a professional for a series of well-lighted close-up photos. Arrange the photos in sequence and write a caption or word explanation to describe the activity in each step.

For some crafts, such as needlework, jewelry, and others, line drawings communicate more information more clearly in less space than photos. Exploded drawings and line shadings for emphasis can show assembly details not visible in even the best photographs. Work with a commercial artist to develop detailed drawings, preferably in a barter exchange for your crafts.

When you are satisfied, try your instructions on several typical, inexperienced housewives, older men, and teen-agers. Hand your photos, written instructions, and materials to someone who has had absolutely no training or background in your craft and ask him or her to complete the example project using only the photos and written information furnished. If these reasonably intelligent "guinea pigs" can put the project together with no stumbles or questions not resolved from the instructions packed with the materials, then you can send out kits. If your trial craftsman encounters difficulty along the way, revise the illustrations, words, or both to clarify the instructions. Remember, a kit buyer cannot ask questions. You must anticipate problems and answer all questions in your instructions. Here's where class instruction and trials pay off. Most kit packagers begin their step-by-step instructions at too high a level. They have forgotten some of the simple steps at the beginning because they do those automatically. Only when the rawest amateur can assemble a project or proceed through the steps to complete all activities without stumbling should you be satisfied with the basic set of instructions.

Second, your instruction folder should show a variety of alternative designs to spark the imagination of the kit buyer. These alternatives can be photographs of complete projects or illustrations in line or wash drawings. Drawings offer the advantage of showing more ideas in less space than photographs, thereby controlling the cost of printing. A number of eye-catching photos can decorate the box if your kit is to be packaged in a printable container. Projects pictured on the box help to sell kits when displayed on your shop counters or in a craft shop. Sparkling idea drawings or photos inside build interest and generate orders for more kits—and your sales expand.

Include a blank reorder form in each kit to encourage the buyer to reorder. Kits with basic materials, such as the dippity-goo kits for crafting flowers and leaves, offer great variety for the accomplished craftsman. But reorders will depend on a neophyte's success in using the first batch of materials. Kits with materials for a specific design, such as a stitchery kit that includes a design printed on backing cloth and the yarn for completing the design, should be pictured on the reorder form or in a folder. Pack the illustrated order form or folder in each kit package. If you include photographs, make sure they radiate professional quality—no snapshots.

Study and restudy the ideas in Chapter 2 for publicizing your kits. By using your skill and showmanship on TV or in a photograph along with a story in your local newspaper, you can gain numerous customers and begin your sales campaign with a minimum cash outlay for advertising. Just make sure your kits are tested and ready for the market before publicity breaks.

Selling materials, special tools, equipment, and instructions by mail are detailed in the other chapters for those specialties.

Chapter 8

TEACHING YOUR CRAFT TO OTHERS
FOR PROFIT

Few professions deliberately expand the number of skilled practitioners and competitors with anything like the missionary zeal of men and women in crafts. As a skilled craftsman you enjoy sharing your love of crafts with others. Contrast this openness with the close-out tactics of state examining boards, union hiring halls, professional societies, and graduate schools for the professions. Crafts can be a joy and a broadening therapy—and teaching spreads the inner gratification that comes from passing along skills and watching others craft projects they are proud to show.

Along with the joy of sharing your skills with beginners and others less skilled, teaching opens a number of alternatives for cashing in on your know-how, skills, and design philosophies.

Teaching in a School System

You can earn a salary or hourly fees as a part-time instructor in a high school or community college adult education program. As a part-time lecturer, you will usually be paid by contact hour—that is, the number of hours you actually conduct classes. A three-hour session at $12/contact hour pays $36 for a once-a-week class. Payment varies according to the school system—lowest for high schools, highest for four-year university classes—with tougher competition for teaching positions as you move up the ladder. Contact hour rates vary from $8 to $18. Salary scales adopted for the school system control the rate rather than the craftsman's reputation or class attendance.

If you are interested in teaching at your local high school or community college, here's how to go about it. If the school system is equipped with craft equipment, such as pottery wheels and kilns, for example, the regular staff may also teach evening classes. Call the school's registrar to see if a class is already offered in your craft. Or watch local newspapers for class offerings. If a class is not offered in your specialty and you know that equipment is available, contact the director of the adult education program. Offer your services along with a proposal that details how you would teach the class. It is as simple as that. If you are qualified, the school may set up a class, publicize it, and check the demand. Registration must reach a minimum level—usually eight to twelve students. If too few students sign up, the class will be canceled. But you can help fill out the registration by telling your friends. Your reputation in the community as a craftsman will help to draw students.

If your craft specialty requires little or no equipment and no class is currently being offered, develop a proposal and contact the director. Stitchery, jewelry, metalcrafting, flowercraft, and many other crafts can be taught with equipment and materials you bring to the classroom yourself. You follow the same steps as before—sell the director on the need for your craft class and promote registration among friends and associates.

When you teach your class, combine techniques with actual practice—this is known as the laboratory technique. Begin by introducing the basics. First, to motivate the interest of your class, show the variety of items the students will be learning to make. Then, demonstrate each basic step from the beginning. If some of your students are already past the beginning stages, your demonstration will serve as a refresher or explain an alternative method. Immediately after your demonstration, start the students working on their own creations. Select a beginning project easy enough to complete by the end of the first session. No amount of lecturing and demonstration will benefit your students as much as their participation. As they craft their first project, circulate to each student in turn. Concentrate on the rank beginners who may appear to be all thumbs or hesitant about starting. Dispense encouragement in great gobs. Get them started off right and they will generate their own enthusiasm. Expect mistakes, but turn each mistake into a learning situation for the stu-

6.   Candlemaker deftly works at final decoration of elaborate candle in a shop set up
in shopping mall in Chicago. (Photo: *Steve White*)

7.   Janet White demonstrates flowercraft to class that builds clientele for materials and kits. Marketing materials affords a better opportunity for sales than selling completed crafts when skills are simple to learn. Persons interested in flowercraft, macramé, and similar crafts often prefer making their own. (Photo: *Steve White*)

8.   Distinctive signature fused into glaze identifies Lorelei Paster as the potter and helps to build a reputation for distinctive crafts. (Photo: *Steve White*)

9. Log House showroom in college-owned Boone Tavern Hotel offers products of Student Craft Industries at Berea College, Kentucky. Woodcrafts are one of six media taught as part of Berea College labor program. (Photo: Joe Clark, *Courtesy of Berea College*)

10. Puzzles and games constructed from wood draw interest from youngsters in Berea College Log House showroom. (Photo: Joe Clark, *Courtesy of Berea College*)

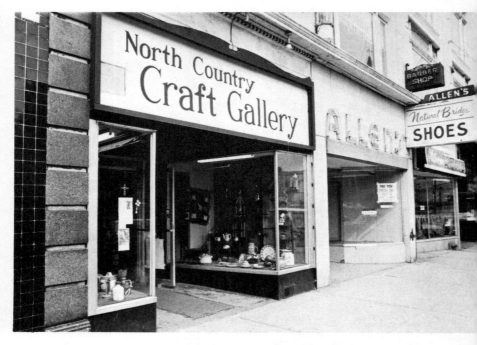

11. Storefront gallery offers crafts produced by associated craftsmen to spread selling costs. Selling direct through an association can increase net income compared to selling through consignment shops or wholesale to private galleries.

(Photo: Gary C. Walts)

12.   Collection of artistic business cards used as selling messages. Artistic, inexpensive cards distributed at arts and crafts fairs and in talks or demonstrations cue follow-up sales or custom assignments. (Photo: *Jim Squires*)

dent. Show each one in turn what he or she is doing wrong and help him or her succeed before going on to the next student. During the opening session answer questions from the students, analyze their problems, and assist them over the hard parts as you demonstrate again and again the right way to get started. Laboratory classes are easy to teach because you minimize lectures and demonstrations and concentrate on getting each student under way on his own project.

At the beginning of the second and succeeding sessions, introduce a new technique or several alternative design ideas. Keep challenging the students to advance and learn new skills—even if they still stumble over the techniques and skills you taught before. Devote part of each classtime to the analysis of student work produced outside of class. One-to-one constructive criticism encourages students to work outside of class. If equipment is limited, set up a sharing schedule that allows each student access to the equipment.

If you have never taught a class before, you will probably learn more than the students. As you teach succeeding classes, you can gauge your introduction of new material to the abilities of the class. Some groups learn faster than others. Although you want to challenge your students, don't make the mistake of most new teachers by shoving new ideas, techniques, and designs at the class too fast. Others may stick to a rigid predetermined schedule. If you find most of the class floundering and unable to complete the projects you have planned, don't hesitate to repeat your demonstration. Or repeat the exercise with a slight design variation if necessary. But concentrate on developing class projects that will enable students to take home something completed. They like to show their accomplishments—actual projects they can display to their friends.

If you have never attended a craft class before, study other teachers. Register for a class at a university or community college and sample teaching techniques—even if the craft is different from your specialty.

Teaching a class in a school system may also start cash flowing from the sale of materials, tools, and equipment. Most school systems will not permit you to sell materials or tools directly to students during class. You can, however, establish yourself as a source where students may buy between classes and after the course is finished. You can do this easily if you already operate a teaching facility, retail shop, or sell crafts from your home. If you don't supply these materials and other necessities, some other craft outlet will benefit from your teaching.

Private Classes in Shop or Home

Fees paid by students for classes taught in your own home or shop can generate more spendable cash than teaching in a school system. Producing craftsmen combine teaching with the operation of a retail shop for selling their own work. Adding tools, equipment, and materials is the next logical step. Students pay to learn craft techniques and to use your expensive tools and equipment. Private classes tend to be less structured; that is, they offer shorter lectures and more bench time than school classes. Attendance is not keyed to a ten-week or six-week schedule. Classes in your own facility may run on for as long as students continue to come. Rank beginners work alongside advanced craftsmen refining their skills or expanding their range of techniques. As a result, laboratory classes in a facility of your own tend to be one-on-one where you work with each student individually and support that one person's needs. Unstructured classes, therefore, tend to be smaller with six or eight teaching stations about maximum.

Examples prove the profitability of private classes.

Rick Olson teaches jewelry design and fabrication, gemstone faceting, and stone cutting in his own shop. Rick started crafting jewelry at the age of eight. Since then, his work has won numerous national awards, including the Masters Trophy at the National Gem Show.

Rick offers lessons laboratory style in continuous sessions. Students do not commit themselves for any specific number of lessons but continue at their own pace. Students learning jewelry design and fabrication begin metalcrafting by soldering small projects using low-cost metals, such as copper and German silver, at first. They progress to sterling silver and gold materials as their skill increases.

Classes meet for two and one-half hours once a week. Rick currently schedules one class in the afternoon and one class in the evening on Wednesdays, Thursdays, and Fridays. Each student pays $6.00 for each lesson at the time he attends. Rick furnishes a completely outfitted bench, a soldering torch, full range of pliers, ring mandrel, shears, scribe—all the tools needed for metalcrafting or preparing patterns and molds for casting jewelry. Including the bench, Rick spends about $120 to equip each teaching station. Tools and equipment are purchased at wholesale prices, as he is a dealer.

Low-cost metals and soldering materials are furnished as part of the basic price for beginning lessons. When a student begins working with more expensive metals and gemstones, he or she buys these materials at competitive prices from Rick. Many times a student may bring his own to class. Major equipment, such as centrifugal casting machines, burnout oven, vacuum pump, rolling mill, grinders, and shears constitute an investment of just under $500. Major equipment is available to students, but not located at each bench. Rick's facilities include space for a maximum of eight students. During classtime he circulates around to each bench to answer questions, demonstrate techniques, offer design suggestions, analyze problems, and encourage students to improve their skills.

"I like to teach students interested in developing their design and craft skills as a hobby or for their personal enjoyment rather than students who want to learn jewelry handcrafting as a money-making profession," Rick says. "There are already too many crude craftsmen who think they are jewelers trying to hammer out a few quick gimmicks for sale at penny prices. Jewelry crafting requires years of practice and design innovation. Jewelry crafting is no quickie way to make a fast buck."

Rick limits his own bench time to crafting custom jewelry commissioned by clients. He designs wedding rings and sets, special mounts for unique gemstones, and gift pieces for clients who return time and again because of his outstanding craftsmanship.

At first he tried teaching a few students in his home, but mass confusion reigned, and students were constantly interrupted. Opening the shop in a nearby business district separated teaching from his own craft production. He still does all of his own work at his custom shop in his home. He pays $180/month rent for the shop that measures roughly 30 x 25, ample room for eight teaching benches and group equipment. On Mondays each week another craftsman uses the shop facilities for teaching classes in faceting. On Tuesdays a different craftsman teaches lapidary. Keeping the shop fully occupied helps to reduce the overhead chargeable to each student. On the two days others use the shop, Rick produces custom jewelry at his home bench.

Teaching builds a customer clientele for tools and materials, both of which are stocked in the shop. He sells tools and equipment for jewelry crafting, faceting, and lapidary. As each jewelry student develops skills, he or she begins to build up her own bench at home. Students turn out projects for criticism during classes. Rick sells tools and equipment at a markup that averages 25 per cent of the retail or list price. He also stocks materials and findings for sale to students and practicing jewelers. Since the shop is easy to find and is located on a busy bus line, his materials and supplies business is growing steadily. Big-ticket items, such as casting machines and laps are sold from a catalogue because he has neither the space nor capital to stock a wide variety of expensive equipment. Orders may be filled in days if a distributor stocks the item locally. Otherwise, two to three weeks' delivery is common and accepted.

Philip Morton, master silversmith and head of The Working Hand Craft Center, mentioned earlier, operates on a different concept. He offers in-depth teaching for aspiring jewelry crafters. He offers a three-year apprentice learn-and-work program for up to eight apprentices at one time. There is no fixed schedule other than the split in a day's activities. During mornings students learn and practice new techniques. Or they experiment with designs. Each student develops a close working relationship with metals and gemstones in learning progressively more complicated techniques. Afternoons are devoted to production of individually designed pieces.

Apprentices pay $400/quarter for their training and use of the bench facilities at The Working Hand Craft Center. "By the end of their first year, apprentices are earning a portion of their tuition from their work," Phil reports. "During the third year, I will usually award full scholarships because the apprentices who stick with the program will be producing salable goods." Pieces that meet Phil's exacting standards of design and quality craftsmanship are sold through the retail shop and other outlets by an agent. "Our retail shop is currently grossing an average of $600/month. But nothing goes to a customer unless I would be willing to have my personal stamp on it," Phil states.

The Working Hand Craft Center is the outgrowth of Philip Morton's desire to establish a combined production-teaching center after spending twenty-five years on the teaching staff at the University of Minnesota. "Students in my classes at the university could learn design and craft techniques, but they had too little opportunity to practice and perfect their skills. The apprentice program combines intensive teaching with learn-by-doing practice where I can see and guide their development. Practice—practice—practice. It's the only way to learn craftsmanship. And I enjoy teaching in depth that way."

Crafts Workshop offers a variety of courses including pottery, macramé, stitchery, weaving, wire jewelry, and wood carving. The Workshop hires specialized teachers in each craft and schedules classes primarily for profit. Rather than offering classes on a continuing basis, each of the courses is structured for eight-week sessions. Students are exposed to a planned sequence of techniques demonstrated by the instructor. Students practice at home and bring any problem encountered to class the following session for criticism.

An instructor is paid $10 for each contact hour, much like the system for teachers in high school or community college systems. Class sizes are limited in those crafts where specific equipment is used. For example, only eight students are accepted for pottery because each student uses his own electric wheel. Class fees for pottery are $85 for the eight-week course—payable in advance. But for macramé, any number of students up to twenty can be accommodated because equipment requirements are minimum. An eight-week course in macramé costs $70.

Structured lecture-demonstration courses in crafts offer less satisfaction than the learn-by-doing laboratory system where students advance at their own pace. Structured sessions must advertise a number of techniques and designs to attract students. However, some students dislike the fast pace of instruction and drop out when they fall behind or fail to receive the individual attention they want and need.

Classes offered on a scheduled basis are paid for in advance. If the student drops out, no tuition is refunded. Such schools offer little incentive for the dedicated craft instructor because: (1) Salary paid by contact hour is likely to be a minimum—less than is paid in school systems. (2) Lecturing and group demonstration are emphasized rather than problem analysis and individual help for each student. Many craftsmen are not equipped by temperament or experience to stand up in front of a class and lecture. (3) Little or no opportunity for follow-up sales of materials and equipment are open to the crafts-man-instructor. This income will be earned by the commercial school as a one-stop source for student supplies, tools, and equip-ment. (4) Little or no opportunity exists for the sale of the instruc-tor's own work or the work of advanced students as an incentive to produce salable goods.

Special Opportunities

Clubs and organizations offer craft classes that open teaching op-portunities for craftsmen interested in expanding their income. Women's clubs, YW-YMCA, and park or recreation departments of local governments sponsor crafts for recreation and to expand the in-terests of their members or the public. These courses favor simple crafts requiring minimum tools, few skills, and low-cost materials. Macramé, papercraft, stitchery, dipping plastic, flower arranging, weedcrafts, and wire jewelry can be adapted for these classes much more easily than the heavy crafts of pottery, ceramics, and metalcrafted or cast jewelry. YW-YMCA organizations are often equipped to offer in-depth craft instruction and cover the full range of crafts.

Breaking into these classes as an instructor calls for initiative on your part. A woman's club or park department might seek you out, but don't count on it. If you are interested in teaching, search out possibilities by contacting organizations yourself, as follows:

Park and recreation departments may be organized under city or county governments with a budget specifically devoted to improving skills and developing hobby interests. Under the auspices of P&R, res-idents swim, play ball, and picnic in park facilities. Some P&R de-partments sponsor Shakespeare in the park gratis, tennis and swim-ming lessons—and craft programs. Do a little homework before tackling the director. For example, obtain a copy of the budget from the city and/or county clerk, pick up a copy of the program for a previous year, ask your library for clippings of class announcements, and possibly visit one or more of the craft facilities. Look specifically at the craft instruction offered in past years. If your investigation turns up a potential opportunity, develop a plan for selling yourself as an instructor. Lay out a program to cover the number of hours in each session and the number of sessions (you will know this from your investigation). Collect samples of your work that fit in with each lesson plan. Develop a sample lesson sheet with written instructions and illustrations for reproduction in black and white on P&R duplicating equipment for class handouts.

When you are ready, write or call the director of the park and recreation department. You will be undertaking a double mission—first, to sell a program, second, to sell yourself as instructor. Ask for an appointment to propose a craft program. A well-organized proposal that includes lesson plans, sample projects, and a schedule of topics puts you head and shoulders ahead of the usual applicant who simply wants to teach. From that point, you can begin discussing times, payment, class sizes, and promotion. Acceptance of your proposal will depend on budgets, previous plans, and facilities. Your reputation, tear sheets of promotion in newspapers or magazines, possibly a book you have written, a list of awards or shows in which you have appeared help to establish your qualifications as a crafts instructor. Emphasize any previous teaching experience in your proposal along with photos of your work and your previous students.

Trudy Broz teaches weedcraft at a series of craft workshops sponsored by a county parks and recreation department. Trudy also operates a shop called The Weed House, where she and an associate sell kits for making seedpod wreaths and candleholders, free-standing dried flower arrangements, straw flower pots, and other innovative and decorative items from weeds, dried flowers, cones, and seed pods.

Trudy began teaching the classes in the fall when weeds, cones, and other natural materials were most abundant. She had taught herself most of what she knew about weeds. Her long-standing interest in the outdoors took her to places where unusual dry materials could be picked at random. Long-stemmed weed pods are available for the gathering in great variety in most localities.

Her first contact was with the director of the Parks and Recreation Department. She had already determined two things: (1) P&R did sponsor free craft classes—weaving without a loom, wire jewelry, and others. (2) P&R did not include classes in weedcraft on their schedule. To learn more about the program, she registered for the class in handweaving. The teacher was experienced in handling the large group and offered a combination of techniques and practice at each lesson.

Trudy picked up one good idea in the class—the instructor used an overhead projector to illustrate specific moves in developing designs for macramé. She actually worked on the plate, and her movements in working with each piece were enlarged and projected onto a near vertical screen. Thus, each of the students could follow the work at her seat. The instructor also used the overhead projector to show design ideas with a pointer to emphasize specific techniques. Trudy filed that idea away for future use on her own. By attending the class, Trudy also learned the following:

❖ Discipline was no problem. Students attending the class were there to learn. There was no credit for the class. If the students lost interest, they simply dropped out.

❖ Progress was slower than she would have liked because the pace of the instruction was keyed to the many slow learners in the class. Many of the students had no previous experience with crafts of any kind. Slow progress could be discouraging, but the instructor kept the quick learners challenged by distributing special assignment sheets to those who finished class assignments early. Slow learners could take the extra work assignments home or simply let them pass.

❖ Students derived great satisfaction from learning and crafting projects they could take home to show their family and friends.

❖ Concerned about being able to stand up in front of a class and teach, Trudy watched and learned how informal such classes could be. She relaxed and could see her role as an instructor much more clearly after attending the six sessions.

Trudy assembled a variety of her work to show the director. Further, she developed a detailed set of lesson plans and made up the finished project that would be completed during each lesson. The last item in her proposal was a list of materials and their cost. Since the lessons were to be offered free, students would be required to buy their materials. During the fall many weeds could be gathered and brought to class. Otherwise, materials were programed to cost less than $.50 per week. When she approached the director with her definitive plan, samples, and cost, he agreed immediately. Although the fall class was planned to begin after school started, Trudy completed arrangements in early summer. Plans for such classes are normally finalized three to four months ahead to permit publication of classes offered and for publicity. Trudy earned $10 per contact hour, and the classes ran two hours per week.

Although she was permitted to sell only the materials required for the class in the parks and recreation program, students soon learned of the location of The Weed House and began showing up to buy additional materials. Thus, she increased the traffic in her shop while spreading the word about using and arranging weeds as a craft.

Summer camps offer another teaching opportunity. Wood carving, leathercraft, beadwork, and macramé are favorite crafts taught at day camps near cities and at boarding camps where children spend one to two weeks at a time. Crafts tend to be simple and are often based on kits. Blanks to be carved for neckerchief slides are popular in Boy Scout camps. Beadwork and leathercraft follow stamped designs and require little real craftwork. As an instructor at a distant camp, you may also double as a counselor, swimming instructor, and cabin attendant. To qualify as a craft instructor for camps, you should be conversant with and skilled in a number of crafts. You apply for these short-time positions usually no longer than six to eight weeks, by searching out the camp directors and writing a letter of application. Look for camps in the classified section of the telephone directory, local newspaper classifieds, travel and recreation sections of Sunday newspaper editions, and by contacting such organizations as the Boy Scouts. Summer camp situations are varied, and craft programs are emphasized in different degrees. Pay for classes in camp will include room and board along with a limited salary—$65/week and up. Your best bet is to search out a range of possibilities and decide which you prefer before applying, starting with the most desirable first. Staffing decisions are usually completed in January or February, so submit your application early.

Extending your craft expertise through the mails poses a completely different mode of profiting from your know-how. The field is open mainly because of the constraints and the variety of talents needed to market crafts instruction by correspondence. Consider these basic requirements: (1) Lesson plans or kit instructions must be written and illustrated in sufficient detail to replace most of an instructor's lecture and to answer questions before they arise. Printing of lesson plans calls for a substantial investment of both time and cash. (2) Attracting customers for correspondence lessons calls for specific mail-order marketing skills. Many potential craftsmen simply believe that teaching crafts by mail is impossible. Others have been burned often by unsatisfactory purchases by mail. Costs of advertising and/or direct mail solicitation increase the initial investment. (3) Mail handling through the post office, the many order forms, records of payments, individual correspondence, and packaging require considerable time and expense if handling is to be prompt, efficient, and satisfactory to students who learn by mail.

Despite these formidable handicaps, at least one opportunity for teaching by mail is being widely exploited by profit-oriented craftsmen. These are the kit packagers. Dipping-plastic kits, weed wreaths, stitchery, and candle-crafting kits are sold by the thousands through the mail. Actual instruction takes a back seat to the kit concept where everything needed comes in a box. Kit sellers must teach basic crafts in enough depth to enable the purchaser to fabricate the specific project or variations, in the case of dipping plastic. Lesson plans are complete for the kit project, but they develop few basic craft skills.

Combined Opportunities

Teaching as a road to craft earnings can be a limited and sometimes frustrating experience because so much appears to go out in terms of preparation and know-how for a small return. If you enjoy teaching and derive pleasure from seeing others learn and develop skills, then the monetary return assumes less importance. However, if you depend on teaching as an important revenue activity, then consider the side benefits available to the teacher who also operates a shop for materials, tools, and equipment, such as Rick Olson.

Offering classes in your own shop will bring in more cash than teaching for a fee in a public school system or other organization. Rick Olson's students generate a gross income of $48 for an afternoon or evening session when eight students pay $6 for a lesson. At $10/contact hour, he would earn only $25—and probably teach a class at least twice as large. Further, he is able to offer at least six classes a week for a potential gross of $288/week. A school system would limit a course offering to one or two sections per week during only a part of the year.

A greater revenue potential is the profit from sales of materials, tools, and equipment. Once a person commits his interest to a hobby, he will spend hundreds—even thousands—of dollars on equipment depending on the craft. The craftsman or hobbyist finds buying his supplies, tools, and equipment convenient at the shop where he learns. Retail markup on tools and equipment will average 25 per cent of the retail purchase price. A 40 per cent markup is common on most materials and supplies. Offering lessons brings customers into contact with a well-stocked store. Offering a full range of supplies for the jewelry craftsman also attracts buyers who become prospective students. Thus, one activity feeds the other.

A shop that offers lessons, materials, and tools may also offer finished craft products for sale to ordinary shoppers. You can offer your own production plus products from students whose work meets your standards, as in the case of Philip Morton. You gain a triple benefit. First, by offering an outlet for their finished work, you attract students and motivate them to learn the skills necessary to produce salable work. Second, as the shop owner, you earn a markup on student work sold. Third, by offering student work for sale, you can show a greater variety of designs and more products to tempt purchasers. Some of the secondary benefits that accrue are the opportunities to promote classes and sales through publicity or advertising. None of these benefits accrues directly to the teacher who holds classes in a school system or other organization.

Teaching crafts opens numerous avenues for promotion and direct sales to groups in person or by mail. People love to learn, so teaching offers a low-key sales route to sell your know-how, finished products, and associated tools and materials. As a craftsman-businessman, you can seek out and exploit several of the teaching opportunities used successfully by craftsmen to increase their spendable income through crafts.

Chapter 9

PUBLISHING YOUR CRAFT KNOW-HOW
AND DESIGNS FOR PROFIT

Craft magazines and books offer a three-pronged opportunity for marketing your designs and technical abilities.

❖ Being published in a national magazine aids in publicizing you and promoting your crafts.
❖ You earn fees for articles and royalties from books.
❖ Photos, drawings, and step-by-step instructions can be restructured and recycled for kits, lesson plans, and teaching materials.

Not only are these three benefits inseparable, one use spurs the development and marketing of the others. Particularly important are the promotion benefits you reap as a nationally recognized craftsman-author.

Promotion activities are more closely detailed in Chapter 2, but look briefly at what happens when your craft know-how appears in print. Paul Merriman brought to market a fountain-action wax pen for free-forming wax to be cast into figures and creative jewelry. To show how the new wax pen functioned, he photographed completed pieces in full color. Then, he wrote and illustrated an article on how to use the pen, including step-by-step photos of the wax pen in use. The color photograph was printed on the cover of *Lapidary Journal*, a gem-cutting, lapidary, and jewelry magazine. Inside, complete with two pages of color photos, the article was reproduced practically as he wrote it. Sales had been lagging, but they immediately jumped and have remained high ever since. A second two-part article showing the wax pen in use appeared in *Gems and Minerals* magazine.

Another color cover photo attracted the attention of readers to the design capabilities of the pen.

Articles in specialized or trade magazines typically return little or no direct cash. Some magazines pay $20 to $40 per printed page for articles complete with photographs and drawings. Other magazines pay nothing, but they do offer the opportunity for publicity. You can use them to establish your reputation. Presumably, if you have a choice, you would prefer to be paid for writing an article. However, if the promotion fall-out from the appearance of an article means more than the immediate cash return, offering an article at no cost to the leading periodical in that field could pay off in sales.

How can you tell whether magazines pay for articles or not? You have two choices: First, consult the *Writer's Market*, a book published annually by *Writer's Digest* Magazine, 9933 Alliance Road, Cincinnati, Ohio 45242. *Writer's Market* details the editorial requirements for almost every magazine and book publisher in the United States. If a magazine pays for articles published, the rate is noted. Indicated rates trend toward the low side generally; that is, if the *Market* reports a magazine pays $50 per page, that will likely be the minimum. A well-written article with professional quality photographs and/or camera-ready artwork will draw a higher rate. Editors reason thus: Any published payment figure will be considered the norm. If a badly prepared article appears "over the transom," but offers something unique in design or technique, editors may develop the article themselves. However, because of the extra work, they offer the author a minimum fee. On the other hand, an article with professional-quality photos, written in a terse, word-conscious style may go directly into production with a minimum of editing. Such articles are worth more—and magazines can up the payment schedule. Editors find it easier to scale payments up rather than down.

The second way to determine payment scales is to write to the magazine and ask. Some magazines publish a short letter or folder describing their editorial and illustration requirements. Types of film, specifications for drawings, and the kinds of articles they prefer are detailed in these authors' folders.

Articles in craft magazines are easy to prepare and sell or place when written to suit a magazine's style and format. Editorial content in specialized craft magazines attracts readers who, in turn, buy products or services from advertisers. A battle between advertising and editorial departments for revenue and nonrevenue pages rages constantly in magazine offices. Like many creative activities, writing for publication takes home a pitifully thin slice of the total dollar pie. Magazine editors constantly look for better material at low prices or for free. In the craft field, many authors feel compensated if their name appears in print. In such an environment, editors are likely to be stingy with their dollars.

Books, on the other hand, pay off handsomely when published and promoted extensively. The burgeoning interest in crafts has fostered an outpouring of books on every conceivable craft. One recent count placed the craft books in print at more than a thousand. While the market continues for new craft books, writing and selling a book are much more difficult than writing and selling magazine articles.

Writing for Magazines

Look first at the two types of magazines interested in craft articles:

First, there are the general magazines that offer varied editorial content. *Woman's Day, McCall's, Popular Mechanics,* and *Better Homes and Gardens* appeal to a varied audience and thereby gain circulations in the millions. Craft articles make up only a small part of these magazines' editorial content. Yet, for accepted manuscripts, payment is tops. Requirements are stiff with the accent on professional quality. These magazines receive so few acceptable craft articles from free-lance writers and/or craftsmen that many of the articles published originate in the magazine's offices. Even if an article is bought from a writer or craftsman, the photographs will almost always be reshot in the magazine's studio or by a commercial photographer. While these magazines offer a high-paying market, the chances of "hitting" remain slim unless you fully understand the magazine's requirements and submit professional-quality work.

Second, specialized magazines cater to the interests of craftsmen working in narrow fields. *Lapidary Journal, Embroiderer's Journal,* and *Handweaver and Craftsman* are typical of magazines that aim directly at the craft fields indicated in their title. Specialized periodicals circulate in much smaller numbers to a limited audience with similar interests. *Lapidary Journal,* for example, is a leading publication in the gemstone field, but its circulation runs under sixty thousand copies monthly. Reduced circulation means lower prices for articles, but special-interest magazines offer a much greater market for well-done articles for two reasons:

❖ A craft magazine devotes its full attention to craft articles.
❖ Since many more magazines are published, the market is much broader.

Editors of specialized craft magazines constantly cry for more good articles—with the emphasis on *good*. More good articles would be forthcoming if the no-pay or low-pay policy were changed, of course. Professional writers cannot afford to write for specialty periodicals when the pay remains low. Thus, the field remains wide open for the craftsman-writer with an eye to the publicity potential of appearing in print. The craftsman who delivers acceptable articles benefits from the sale of materials, kits, equipment, or other craft-related products.

The terms "professional-quality photographs" and "camera-ready drawings" appear throughout this chapter. These two requirements draw more attention among editors of specialized magazines than the writing. Editors typically expect to rewrite most articles submitted by craftsmen because the articles are either poorly written or are far too long. If you are gifted with a flair for writing as well as creative design, you can count on a welcome reception by editors.

Photographs of professional quality are well lighted, clear, in sharp focus, and printed on 5 x 7 or 8 x 10 paper for black and white reproduction. Color photographs should be submitted as transparencies, preferably in 2¼ x 2¼ size, though 35mm slides are acceptable if sharp and bright. Along with good technical quality, photographs must show finished crafts or projects and progressive steps in crafting the projects. Photographs must communicate graphically; unless they do, you can count on a rejection. Finished pieces, particularly, must be interesting and eye catching. As a reader flips through the magazine, your photographs must catch his eye instantly. The finished piece must appeal to the reader as unique in design or promise to explain a technique that expands the reader's skill. Snapshots taken without regard to lighting, with confusing and distracting backgrounds, or printed by the corner drugstore will not generally be acceptable.

Camera-ready drawings are line illustrations drawn in black ink on white paper ready for shooting to make plates for printing. Callouts and dimensions may be hand-lettered directly on the drawing if that is the magazine's style. If type callouts are used in the magazine, drawings should show only arrows to specific parts. Then, on a transparent overlay, callouts or dimensions may be handwritten as a guide. During production of the article in the magazine's editorial office, type will be set according to your handwritten notations and stripped onto the drawing at the locations indicated on your overlay. Examine the magazine for style of drawings used and whether callouts are hand-lettered or set in type. Don't attempt to set type and paste it in position yourself. The magazine will determine the final size of your drawings and set type to compensate for any change in size. Sharp, crisp linework and line shading are the important elements of camera-ready drawings.

Before developing articles for any magazine, study several issues of the magazine and others in the field. For example, if you intend to submit photographs of completed craft projects, examine the photographs that appear in such magazines as *Craft Horizons, Woman's Day,* and the many idea books on handcrafts published by *McCall's, Better Homes and Gardens,* and others. You will find the latter in annuals, quarterlies, and one-shot publications on large newsstands in your area. Most of the photographs are taken in the studios of the magazines themselves or assigned to photographers and taken in their studios for one big reason—they can control quality and shoot better photos than those available from the craftsman or run-of-the-mill commercial photographer.

❖ Examine the lighting for clues to interest and sparkle. You can see how individual pieces were lighted by examining the shadows.

❖ Look at the backgrounds. Most projects will be photographed against a paper backdrop that permits a backlight to wash out many of the sharp shadows. A backdrop gently curving upward from the base on which a piece is resting eliminates any distracting base lines and distractions on a bench or in a room. Photos taken with crafts in position on a wall, being worn, or on display on shelves will be lighted to highlight the setting as well as the project itself.

❖ Compare any photographs you may have taken with those

reproduced in these top magazines. If your photos do not compare favorably, your article goes to bat in an editorial office with one strike against it.

Photographs appearing in many of the specialized publications will not compare favorably with those in the top periodicals for only one reason—the editors could not obtain the top-quality photos they would prefer within their limited budgets. Thus, when you submit really good, professional-quality photos, the chances of your article being accepted are magnified several times over. Sharp, graphically communicative photos immediately condition the editor to consider your article favorably.

Detail step-by-step photographs call for different composition and lighting. Construction or technique photos should show some particular bit of expertise, a direction not easily described in words, or an interim assembly step not visible in the finished project. Detail photos must be close-ups with minimum background distractions. A problem in taking close-ups of jewelry or other small crafts involves focus and depth of field. Many jewelry photos, for example, are taken from 8 to 12 inches away. Such extreme close-ups require expert lighting and a camera that stops down to f-32 if possible. Such pin-point openings add greater depth of field and permit more of the work area to remain in sharp focus when enlarged. Lighting becomes critical to bring out the glint or color of gemstones and other small work. Detail close-ups should emphasize the activity under way and communicate the unique directions for completing the specific step illustrated.

Some of the best step-by-step photographs are published in *Popular Mechanics* magazine. Examine project-building photos for examples of focusing on the idea being communicated, the lighting, and how close the work is to the camera. Assure good focus in close-ups by using a camera with a ground glass focusing plane, such as one of the press-type cameras or a camera with through-the-lens focusing. Examine one or more of the photography books written for your camera for tips and suggestions on how to take good close-ups. Since good, professional-quality photographs mean so much to the success of an article, plan to spend the necessary time to learn the skills you need to take good photos or develop a working relationship with a professional photographer.

Drawings, preferably in camera-ready form, also aid in communicating step-by-step information. Many magazine editors prefer drawings because they communicate more information in less space than photographs. If your creative skills include an ability to sketch or draw in line, put these talents to use illustrating craft articles. Again, examine the magazines you are aiming for to discern the type of drawings used for illustrations.

Writing the Craft Book

While magazine articles aid in promoting your crafts, kits, materials, equipment, and accessories, craft books generate a continuing income directly. Good craft books sell in fabulous quantities—ten, twenty, forty, on up to one hundred thousand copies over a period of six to twelve years. Craft books remain in print and are reissued periodically as sales continue. Writing a book can be a long-term investment that pays off much like an annuity.

When you write a book and sell it to a reliable publisher, the division of labor works out like this: You furnish the ideas, words, illustrations, and photographs for the book. The publisher pays for all costs of setting type, making plates for the photos (some in color), printing an initial quantity (usually 5,000 copies), binding, stocking, and marketing. You risk your time and whatever costs may be involved in photographs and/or drawings. The publisher risks a major sum of his capital to bring your work to market. The usual split is 10 per cent to the author, 7½ per cent of the cover price on a paperback. Out of the remaining 90 per cent, 40 to 50 per cent goes to the booksellers and wholesalers. The publisher retains 40 to 50 per cent to cover investment in the book and to pay for warehousing, marketing, and distributing the book. Some publishers pay an increasing royalty after the initial print order has recouped make-ready cost.

As an example of how you can benefit, consider the craft book that retails for $8.95. An initial print order of 5,000 copies generates a potential gross of $44,750. As a single author, you would gain a royalty at 10 per cent of $4,475 over the period the 5,000 copies are sold. If your book contract calls for a royalty of 12½ per cent on copies beyond the initial 5,000, your take from a second 5,000-copy print order would amount to $5,594.

Royalties are paid in two steps. Ordinarily, you can expect a small advance against royalties to be paid when you submit an acceptable manuscript with all illustrations. A typical advance is $2,000 against future royalties. You receive nothing more from the publisher (except requests to read proofs and return them overnight) until the book appears in final print and begins selling. Book sales are typically reported for six-month periods—usually January through June and July through December. However, an accounting of sales and payment of royalties may not appear in your mailbox until three to five months after the close of the sales period. For the sales period of January through June, you will probably receive a royalty statement the following September or October. Unless your book sells exceptionally well, the first royalty statement may show a deficit—and no cash. Royalties earned are first charged against any advance you may have received. Also, the publisher may withhold a reserve fund, typically 10 to 20 per cent of the royalties earned, as a hedge for paying refunds if books are returned from booksellers. After that you begin to earn new dollars from your book at more-or-less regular six-month intervals. And the royalty earnings may continue for years with craft books.

If you critically examine the craft books published in your field, you may wonder why some ever saw print. Others will be fountains of information with facts, ideas, and know-how cascading from the pages. Some of the most lavishly printed books in large size and with pages and pages of color offer few new and original ideas. Other less pretentious volumes offer original and innovative techniques, new tools, and creative design ideas. Craft books sell year after year when they challenge the serious craftsman to improve techniques, productivity, and designs. These books inspire the serious craftsman to enlarge his or her horizons and to improve the craft. Unless your book offers something original and truly unique, it is unlikely to achieve wide distribution and remunerative sales. Therefore, the opportunity of writing a craft book is not one open to every craftsman. However, if your designs inspire others, if your techniques and tricks of the trade you've developed are truly innovative and offer a step forward —even a breakthrough—then you owe it to yourself and to your craft associates to collect those ideas and know-how into a book. Here's how you can go about creating your craft book:

You have already determined that you have something important to say in your craft field. You have probably surveyed other books to see how they treat subjects related to yours. Look again—this time for the mix between words, drawings, and photos. Just as with articles for magazines, you'll find many photos of impressive finished examples of crafts to inspire the reader. A good how-to craft book will also include detailed directions for crafting similar items—selecting materials, step-by-step drawings or photos to illustrate difficult techniques, a backup section with reference tables, possibly a "Glossary of Terms," and a full range of ideas to challenge even experienced craftsmen. Not all of the photos need show your own work. A book blooms with versatility when the outstanding work of a number of craftsmen is pictured.

At this stage the idea of developing a book may appear overwhelming. Just as learning and practicing a major craft, a book isn't written overnight. You learn and practice one craft technique and go on to the next. So it is with a book. You write one chapter at a time. By breaking the task into small pieces, you find each new part or chapter exciting and rewarding. But you need a plan—to market the book and to complete it on schedule.

First, recognize that most nonfiction books are written only after a contract is offered and accepted. Writing a complete book without finding a publisher could be mighty frustrating. But if you wrote part of a book and found no publisher, your frustration and production time lost would be easier to accept. Thus, you should plan to interest a publisher before embarking on a complete book.

Second, to interest a publisher, you need a proposal. Your book proposal outlines the contents in detail and includes a plan for developing your book, samples of your writing, and a schedule. Attach your credits—craft awards, gallery presentations, a résumé of your accomplishments in the craft field, and a brief summary of your training and craft background. The purpose of this section is to satisfy an editor's questions about your credentials—your right to lecture to or advise other craftsmen.

An outline of the book you have in mind helps you sort out and organize the pieces. Attack one section or chapter at a time. Don't worry about the order at this point. On separate pieces of paper, jot down the idea, technique, or other information that you believe belongs in your book. These are your building blocks. Brainstorm for ideas, but don't feel you must generate all the ideas in one evening. Generating ideas for your book could extend over weeks—even months. Writers have been known to jot down ideas for several different books as ideas pop into their minds. They chuck these ideas into different drawers or file folders. Eventually one of the ideas begins to assume the proportions of a book, and the writer is off and running. You can do the same with your ideas. Don't worry about sorting them out immediately. Instead, build a backlog of ideas from your teaching, talks with other craftsmen, or from experimenting with new ideas at your bench.

When you have accumulated a number of ideas, sort them into piles according to content. These piles may represent chapters in your book. Try for at least twelve chapters but no more than twenty, although there are few rules on this point. When you are satisfied that the ideas in one stack are related, arrange them into a logical sequence. Just as you started crafting simple projects and graduated to more complex items as you gained experience, begin a chapter with the simplest materials and work up to the most complicated designs and techniques. Branch off to alternative designs or techniques at appropriate points rather than holding all alternatives to the end. When you are satisfied with the order of subjects, list these ideas in outline format. *Voilà!* You have an outline for one chapter of your book. Repeat the process of organizing and outlining until you finish all chapters.

Now, repeat the organization process for the chapters. Select the one chapter that offers basic or introductory material as the opening chapter. Follow that chapter with another that builds on information presented in the first chapter. Continue on through the book until you reach the reference tables or appendix. You develop the index later when page proofs are available. You may find yourself shuffling through the line-up time after time until you find just the right sequence. When you are satisfied, list the chapter titles. You have just outlined your craft book. Now you know where each type of material fits and the order your ideas will follow.

An editor will want to see samples of your writing, photographs, and drawings before deciding to go ahead. An editor first examines the potential of the title and its place in the craft field. Since there is hardly a craft field in which another book has not already been published, he will examine your book for differences in content and approach. His question: What does your book offer that is not available in other existing volumes? If your outline passes those hurdles, the editor will assess your capabilities for developing the book—writing style, photographs, and drawings. Plan to submit from one to four sample chapters complete with photos and drawings, preferably ones that offer a variety of material and illustrations. While you may consider the complete development of several chapters an imposition, remember that a few chapters are easier to write than an entire book.

Your proposal should also include a time schedule indicating when the completed manuscript could be ready for editing. Submitting a proposal with these elements—outline, sample chapters, credits, and a time schedule for writing the book will brand you as a professional to be considered seriously. If your interests run to marketing, you may also include a letter briefly outlining your ideas on why your book is needed, who will likely buy it, your estimate of the size of the potential market, and why you decided to write the book. An editor considers the market for every book published. If you provide a major part of this analysis, his job will be easier—and a decision in your favor more likely.

Stories are legion about books that have been rejected by ten, twenty, or more publishers and gone on to establish sales records. Therefore, if the first publisher who looks at your book sends it back, put it in the mail again. The *Writer's Market* lists most of the publishers in the United States along with a brief rundown on the types of books they publish. You wouldn't send a craft book to a publisher who issues only drugstore paperbacks or to a publisher who specializes in children's books (unless your craft book was aimed at the children's market). Many publishers offer both fiction and nonfiction titles. Some specialize in craft books. Look for the publishers of craft books on your shelf; they could be good prospects. The point is—if you have developed a good craft book and you know it will benefit other craftsmen in your field, keep trying until you find a publisher.

Publishers are notoriously slow about returning a manuscript. One month is common. Two months are also common. But if a publisher holds your proposal for more than two months, drop him a note. Ask for a decision and close by suggesting a telephone conference if he has any questions. Offer to send additional material if that will help him to make up his mind. However, if the publisher is not going to publish your book, you want to get it back. Be sure to enclose a self-addressed stamped return envelope when submitting manuscripts to assure return.

When a publisher decides to publish your book, he will offer a contract. Although the contract will appear to be a standard form printed with blanks to be filled in, remember—there is no such thing as a standard book contract. Every publisher writes his own. The important elements are:

* How much is the advance?
* What is the royalty schedule?
* How much time will you have to complete the book?
* How many free copies will you receive?

Of all the elements, the royalty schedule is the most important. That is, what percentage of the retail price of the book will you receive? At the time a contract is drawn up, the final price of the book will seldom be known. Hence, the emphasis on percentages. You can expect a different royalty for books sold through trade channels (booksellers) and books sold through the mail and through book clubs. Due to higher marketing costs, book-club and mail-order sales yield only 5 per cent of the gross to the author. If you operate a store, teaching facility, or gallery, make sure the contract does not prohibit you from selling your own books obtained at a 40 per cent or higher discount directly from the publisher. Before signing a book contract, you should ask a friendly lawyer to review the terms or engage a literary agent.

Collaboration

Experience and professionalism pay off in publications just as in craft design and fabrication. An alternative to writing your own books is collaborating with a writer and/or photographer. A gifted and innovative craftsman may rate only as an amateur writer and photographer. An ideal combination pairs a talented craftsman with an equally competent writer/photographer. If a book idea and plan are sound but are not supported by professional quality writing and photography, the book may never see print.

Examine your craft work and your interests objectively. Most craftsmen find that they lack the talent or discipline for writing. Collaborating with a writer/photographer often makes sense for both the craftsman and the writer. Both function at their highest skill. Further, the writer knows the ropes about magazine and book markets and can usually put a book together in a fraction of the time required by a nonwriting craftsman.

If you decide to collaborate with a writer and/or photographer, make sure you and he or she understand these ground rules:

❖ You will decide how to split the royalties. Normally, a craftsman and a writer-photographer split fifty-fifty as the simplest solution. If the craftsman also supplies drawings and photographs, the split may be two thirds/one third or three quarters/one quarter with the craftsman taking the big cut because he or she contributes more to the final result. If camera-ready drawings are bought from a third person, out-of-pocket costs are usually shared in the same proportions as the royalty split.

❖ Decide who is to perform each function. The craftsman will obviously make the crafts to be photographed and supply the expertise. The writer/photographer develops the outline and proposal with the craftsman's active participation, shoots the photographs, and writes the copy. The craftsman checks everything for accuracy. Out-of-pocket costs for film, enlarging paper, and processing are normally shared. Each provides whatever equipment is needed to support his own activities. The craftsman supplies material for the crafts, as they will remain his or her property after photography. The writer/photographer works in his own studio and furnishes whatever photographic equipment may be needed—including photo lamps.

❖ Work out a mutually satisfactory work schedule—evenings and weekends if you are both part-timers, or some regular time during the day. Determine at the outset how much time each can devote to the book project. Timing is less critical when developing the proposal, but a fixed time for completing the book will become part of a contract when it is signed.

Ordinarily, a written agreement prior to signing a contract is not necessary. If you should opt for a formal agreement, engage an attorney and do it right. Otherwise, the terms for splitting the royalties can be written into any book contract that develops, and you both sign as coauthors. The publisher or literary agent divides the royalties according to the contract and sends each coauthor his share. If a literary agent is involved, the royalties remaining after the agent has deducted his 10 per cent off the top would be split according to the contract.

Collaborating on articles may take a different tack. As noted earlier, articles in special craft publications either pay nothing or minimal page rates. A professional writer will not be interested in collaborating with no gain in sight. If your interest in publicizing your craft activities relates to sales of craft products, materials, or equipment, you might consider subsidizing a writer who can deliver. If the publication pays for articles, allow the writer to retain full payment for articles published. You gain the benefit from the publicity through sales of your crafts, tools, or materials.

Chapter 10

SELLING INNOVATIVE EQUIPMENT, MATERIALS, AND SUPPLIES

Creative craftsmen constantly originate new ideas for special tools, new materials, and better ideas for working in their specialty. But it is one thing to invent and develop something new or better and quite another to manufacture it at a cost that permits it to be sold profitably in quantity at a competitive price. Manufacturing and marketing plans for products aimed at a specialized market do not spring forth full blown. They develop gradually.

Selling Innovative Equipment

When you have developed a new tool or piece of equipment, how do you market it? The following steps outline the major functions involved in developing and marketing new craft tools or equipment:

Test Marketing—Prototypes of your equipment, probably hand-made, should be tried and tested by other craftsmen—your friends, the head of a shop you know, a teacher of your craft in the community, or a knowledgeable craftsman out of town. You're looking for two kinds of information at this point. What are the problems, if any, of using the tool or equipment? What is the user's opinion of the market potential? In other words, if such a tool were available on the market, would he buy it and at what price?

Market Identification—Where and to whom would production tools or equipment be sold? You need to find out who will buy it and attempt to determine the size of the market. You'll also want to determine if there are competitors in the field offering similar tools and equipment.

Production Planning—If you elect to go ahead with production, how would the product be manufactured? What would the investment costs be for special tooling and equipment? How much of the product could be purchased as standard parts? Costs must be estimated precisely for pricing. Once these figures are determined, additional test marketing might be necessary to probe for price resistance.

Marketing—More than simple selling is involved in marketing your product once it is manufactured. You'll consider packaging—colorful outer packages if it is to sell from a shelf or sturdy boxing if you plan to ship through the mails. Costs of packaging for some products equal the cost of the contents, so a printed box vs. a label stuck on a box offer options in styling and cost. Promotion may be through demonstration, advertising, publicity, and industry shows. The best routes will be determined by the product. Pricing and discount schedules compatible with the trade are involved in marketing through dealers and distributors. Finally, will the product be sold through some dealer network, individually and through the mail, or a combination of both? If sold through dealers, how do you find them?

Once you have developed a new tool, innovative equipment, or special materials, two options are open to you: Market the product yourself or license your development to an existing manufacturer, dealer, or specialty outlet for a royalty. Generally, consider these guidelines when examining the trade-offs:

License and Royalty—Licensing is available mainly to inventors of patented tools or equipment. Without a patent you have little protection against appropriation of your development. Licensing will net you about 5 per cent of the gross sales in royalties. If sales are at the manufacturer's level, the 5 per cent is figured on that gross, not the retail value. But note this—royalties paid through licensing agreements are considered as capital gains which qualify for special income tax treatment. When you contract to license your development, you invest none of the cash for manufacture, and you are not involved in marketing. Your responsibilities end with the delivery of a tested and proved prototype with detail drawings.

Contracting with an outsider to manufacture and market your patented invention poses hazards, however.

First, you gain only royalty income as provided in the contract.

Second, you lose control over the product unless the contract includes an escape clause. If the manufacturer chooses not to promote and market your invention aggressively, there is little you can do unless your contract specifies that a minimum number of units must be sold each year to keep the contract active. Minimum performance guarantees lean toward minimums, as a manufacturer hesitates to commit to a large number without actually testing the market. Therefore, even with a minimum number, the sales could be far less than if you marketed the product.

Third, you gain only the financial benefit from having originated the tool or equipment. With no involvement in the manufacture or marketing, you gain none of the potential earnings from those activities or any corollary return, such as developing and selling related articles using the tool or equipment as a prop.

Manufacture and Marketing—You may choose to manufacture your development and market it yourself whether it is patented or not. If the tool or equipment is not patented, you may gain an advantage over your competition and market your product more aggressively by doing it yourself. If creative crafts interest you more than the business of manufacturing and marketing, then you may prefer to let specialists handle the noncreative details.

Patenting a new invention takes time and money. A relatively simple patent costs an average of $1,500 to $2,500. Further, as long as five years may elapse between application and final award. A quick patent with little or no conflict of claims may be granted in as few as eighteen months, but don't count on it. An initial search for prior art in the Patent Office, as ordered by a patent attorney, will cost $100. Patent attorneys charge by the hour, and you can figure on spending $1,000 to $1,200. The initial search and analysis of the findings by a specialist in patent law can usually determine whether your invention is patentable or not. If the search discloses that prior patents cover developments close to yours, the added expense of applying for and being turned down or negotiating for claims that do not conflict with prior claims may not be worth the cost. The more complicated the application and processing, the higher the cost because more time is involved.

Two cases may help to clarify the issues involved in patenting an invention and marketing it by license and royalty agreement vs. engaging in the functions of manufacturing through marketing.

The Mini-Vac is a patented vacuum device for casting jewelry invented by Dr. Billy Hudson, first for his own use and then for sale. Dr. Hudson works as a physicist at the Lawrence Laboratories in Livermore, California. His hobby is casting jewelry, mainly for his own use. For quality cast jewelry, molten metal must reach every tiny detail of a design left in the mold when wax is burned out.

Two systems in general use assure that metal reaches all parts of the mold. One is a centrifugal machine that whirls the flask in a circle. Centrifugal force throws the molten metal into tiny cavities. These machines are not only expensive but are potentially unsafe. A second method uses vacuum to draw the molten metal into the mold cavity. But pumps capable of drawing a vacuum quickly are also expensive. Either machine costs upward of $250 with good ones exceeding $300.

Drawing on his working knowledge of physics, Dr. Hudson devised a system for heating one-fourth cup of water in a pressure sphere until steam replaces all or most of the air. Closing the valve on the sphere's outlet excludes any air from re-entering the sphere as the steam condenses to water when the sphere cools. Result: a sphere with a few drops of water inside and nothing else, a vacuum controllable by a gate valve in a line to a casting flask. As molten metal pours into the flask, the valve is opened and the vacuum in the sphere pulls the metal into the mold.

Dr. Billy Hudson elected to turn over the manufacturing and marketing of the Mini-Vac to Technical Specialties International, Inc., a development and distribution company with a full line of jewelry metalcrafting and casting tools, supplies, and materials. Dr. Hudson recognized two facts: first, manufacturing and marketing are two completely different skills from inventing or designing jewelry. Further, he had no desire to discontinue his career as a physicist. Second, a smaller slice of a big pie can often represent more dollars than a bigger slice of a small pie.

The contract negotiated between Dr. Hudson and TSI incorporates these provisions: TSI enjoys exclusive rights to manufacture and market the Mini-Vac for the full seventeen years during which the patent is in force providing a minimum of one thousand units are sold each year. Dr. Hudson put up none of the cash required to produce the Mini-Vac in quantity and market it. TSI spent just over $5,000 in tooling and one-time costs to get the Mini-Vac into quantity production. During the first year TSI allocated $3,000 for promotion of the device, which retails for $79.50. Later, a smaller, simpler version was developed to sell for $34.95 as an expansion of the product line.

Another example is the Fetty-Nielsen Macramé Loom, which is a patented, portable wood and plastic device to simplify holding and mounting work as knotting and designs in macramé progress. That the loom was granted a U.S. patent attests its innovative design. Although Joan Fetty's husband is an attorney, they elected to process the patent application with the help of a patent attorney specializing in patent law—and recommend that others do the same.

Rather than license their Macramé Loom to a manufacturer or distributor, Joan Fetty and her mother, Mrs. Nielsen, decided to produce and market the loom themselves. They decided on this course despite six offers to license their loom that appeared out of the blue once the patent was announced in the *Official Gazette* published by the U. S. Patent Office. Their reasons for deciding to produce and market the loom center around the following:

They were dedicated to promoting macramé through design and do-it-yourself articles in a variety of craft magazines and believed they could overcome any deficiencies in business acumen with enthusiasm and spirit. They wanted the loom promoted and distributed actively and felt they were better qualified for that job than anyone else. "There's no way you can buy personal interest and enthusiasm for a product," Joan Fetty reported.

Joan systematically worked through each of the steps necessary in bringing a new craft tool to market. You can retrace with her the steps noted earlier in this chapter to see how you would bring a new craft tool or piece of equipment to market.

Test marketing of the Macramé Loom began when the Fettys built a dozen prototypes in two sizes—one 8 x 13½ inches and the other 13½ x 16 inches. They asked friends to try the looms. They loaned several more to centers for the handicapped where macramé was used as therapy. Other looms went to teachers who used them in their craft classes. Magazine editors were asked to run the prototype looms through their product test for evaluating new products. Opinion was about equally divided as to the proper size, so they elected to produce both. Later sales confirmed the fifty-fifty split in opinion, as the two sizes sell about equally. Further, reaction from the tests appeared generally favorable. From the collected data, they estimated the size of the market at ten thousand looms to be sold over a period of five or six years.

Market identification was easy because Joan Fetty had been developing articles and designs for macramé projects and submitting them to such magazines as *Creative Crafts, McCall's Needlework and Crafts,* and other magazines for years. The looms would replace the unhandy styrofoam and pin setups used by most macramé weavers.

Production planning came harder because neither Joan nor her mother knew much about making products in large quantities. However, by asking questions, picking the brains of their friends, and comparing costs between contract bids, hiring help to work in their basement, and buying looms complete, they settled on a middle course. They elected to buy the materials and deliver them to a handicapped center for assembly. One plastic part for the loom was stamped from sheet plastic. The one-time cost for the stamping die came to $75. Originally the looms were assembled with nails, but by contracting for 2,500, the handicapped center invested in a power stapler that cut costs even more. Contracting for assembly of the loom eliminated the sticky problems of payrolls, withholding taxes, workmen's compensation, insurance, zoning violations if they attempted to set up shop in their basement, and investing in machinery.

Marketing overlapped production planning because the 2,500-lot size was dictated by the minimum order quantity for cardboard cartons. In that quantity boxes cost $.25 each, printed with their own design. A designer developed a logo and design for the box at a cost of $40, and the box printer charged $70 for a one-time plate cost preparatory to printing the boxes.

Distribution, they decided, would be direct to mail-order customers or through dealers, and their prices were set accordingly. The small loom is priced at $6.50 and the large one at $9.95. To simplify collection of postage and packaging expenses, mail-order customers pay an additional $1 to cover shipping west of the Rockies and $1.25 to addresses east of the Rockies. A loom shipped to California costs $.80 to $1.10 depending on size. A large loom shipped to eastern states costs $1.45. Costs average out to about $1 or $1.25, possibly a little more, but the convenience of the two charges compensates for added figuring and any need for refunding excess postage.

When looms are sold directly to retail outlets, the price is reduced 40 per cent from list, standard for the industry. Retailers pay for shipping. Jobbers and distributors buy looms for resale to retailers at discounts from list of 50 and 10. This dual discount translates to a net 55 per cent discount or a yield to the Fettys of $2.93 for the small loom and $4.48 for the large loom. Direct materials and labor run just about half of these figures for the production of looms. Pricing was established after producing several test quantities to determine the effect of the learning curve on labor times.

Joan Fetty takes delivery of the looms fully assembled and packed in the cartons they furnish. In fulfilling mail orders, she affixes labels on individual boxes and hauls them to the neighboring post office. Quantity shipments to retailers and distributors are further boxed in a standard-size container purchased without printing. The size of the bulk container varies with the number and size of looms shipped to a single address.

The most effective means of selling has been the development of product news releases. Joan Fetty sends out a photo of the loom along with a product description to the editors of magazines and newsletters. To date, she has sent out nearly one hundred releases, some to magazines as far afield from crafts as gardening and recreation magazines. Newsletters for organizations in physical therapy, park districts, and others with even the remotest interest in macramé received the releases.

Following that cycle, Joan developed feature articles showing macramé designs and using a loom as part of the step-by-step illustrations. The source of the looms was neatly woven into the articles. Once the pump was primed initially, they found orders flowing in from friends of original buyers.

The Fettys also advertised in *Creative Crafts* and *Recreation* and mailed flyers to hospital gift shops, handicapped centers, parks and recreation boards, and school craft teachers. Mailing lists of these categories were purchased from name list brokers (see Appendix). Retail outlets, dealers, and distributors were picked up when they responded to the publicity and advertising.

Two further outlets developed as a result of their advertising and publicity. One catalogue mail-order house added the looms to their catalogue. But instead of buying the looms and stocking them, the mail-order house sends addresses to the Fettys for drop shipment. The catalogue house pays the postage, but earns the 40 per cent discount. The General Services Administration requested a proposal for sale of the looms to veterans hospitals and other institutions engaged in therapy. To obtain a GSA contract, the Fettys had to agree to sell the looms at the lowest price they were offered to any other buyers, essentially the 50 and 10 per cent discount. Further, GSA inspectors evaluated their production capability and examined their operations in detail to assure compliance with all labor-protection legislation. They passed, and the GSA listed the looms in their catalogue of items available for purchase by schools and hospitals. Individual orders filter in from all parts of the United States and possessions for the looms as a result of this no-cost listing.

More than five thousand of the looms were sold within eighteen months. They are well ahead of their target schedule for selling ten thousand in five years, as the sales rate is increasing month by month. If your craft equipment lends itself to marketing through similar means, you can learn from the tried and proved ideas found successful by Joan Fetty, a mother of young children who works at her craft programs part time.

Marketing Unpatented Craft Tools and Materials

Both the Mini-Vac and the Macramé Loom were patented. The designers could choose between offering the products for license and royalty or producing and marketing the products themselves. If your unique craft tool, equipment, or materials are not patentable, you have little choice but to make and sell the items yourself. Unless you know a manufacturer or distributor personally, your ideas may be appropriated without patent protection. Nevertheless, wide-open opportunities exist for earning cash from the development and marketing of unique tools and materials.

Two businesses founded on the development and marketing of unique tools and materials illustrate the success principles of making money from the sale of craft tools, equipment, and supplies.

The Pourette Company of Seattle, Washington, supplies craftsmen all over the world by mail, through 1,300 dealers and their retail stores. The company began in 1952 when Mrs. Leonard Olsen asked her son to make a reusable round candle mold to replace the makeshift milk cartons and cottage cheese containers she had been using. Sons Don and Ray Olsen operated a heating system installation firm that manufactured sheetmetal heating ducts. Using the firm's sheetmetal equipment, Ray rolled a tin-plated sheet to a uniform circular cross-section with a mite of a taper, soldered the joint and smoothed it so it wouldn't leave a mark. Mrs. Olsen's cylindrical candles attracted attention among friends, and a new craft-based business was under way.

In one recent year the Olsen's Pourette Company sold 105,000 metal molds to candle crafters. The former heating-duct shop now turns out metal molds exclusively, and the company has expanded into more space for handling the accessories, supplies, waxes, and various tools and equipment for candle crafting. Pourette employs fifty-one persons from sheetmetal workers to shipping clerks. Candle wax arrives in carload lots from a major oil company.

Pourette grew to a world-wide candle-craft company due to its specialty—fabricating sheetmetal molds. Consider these proved business builders from the Olsens' experience to help build your craft supply business:

❖ A hardbound book called *Modern Art of Candle Creating* was written early to satisfy demands for instructions on home-crafting candles. The book has gone through five printings and sold more than twenty thousand copies through bookstores and Pourette's mail-order catalogue.

❖ A fifty-page loose-leaf catalogue packaged in a folder with a clear window shows brightly colored candles on the inside. Thus, one color reproduction serves double duty. Individual items can be added, deleted, repriced, or rephotographed without affecting other pages in the loose-leaf format. The Olsens figure the flexibility for constantly updating and expanding the catalogue more than compensates for the added time spent in collating.

❖ Free classes in candle crafting continue at the Seattle retail store. Class members test new products and alert the Olsens to new candle-craft needs. "Creative candlers are using free-form molds, new and unusual containers such as shells, driftwood, and burls plus new techniques for decoration that keep us on our toes," according to Don Olsen.

❖ Pricing follows the usual 40 per cent from list for retail stores, and 50/10 for distributors. The retail markup taken on mail orders pays for the added expense of filling small orders, with a profit left over.

❖ The Pourette Company dealer network and mail-order list was built with patience and small ads appearing in craft magazines (see Appendix). Ads offered the metal molds first. Later ads featured free copies of "The Candle Cauldron" (a monthly newsletter that has been discontinued), a catalogue, or one of the new developments such as a candle sling kit or a felt-lined horizontal bench for supporting candles during decoration. Every reply was added to the growing mail-order customer list. Dealers responded to the same ads or were signed up at industry trade shows. Articles on candle crafting also appeared in trade magazines, such as *Profitable Craft Merchandising* and *Craft, Model & Hobby Industry* (see Appendix for addresses).

In addition to being innovative, creative craftsmen, Ray and Don Olsen recognized the necessity for multiple thrust in marketing through the mail, in their own retail store, and their 1,300-dealer network.

Craftsmen look eagerly for new and better ways to extend the frontiers of their special craft. Bill Garrison, an innovative craftsman-technician-designer, refuses to be bound by traditional tools and materials. A recent book, *Handcrafting Jewelry: Designs and Techniques,** describes techniques for using many of his new tools and materials.

Much of Bill's continued dissatisfaction with the current state of the arts stems from his engineering background and his training as a metallurgist. One of his most popular tools is the prong-bending pli-

* Published by Henry Regnery Company, Chicago, 1972.

ers, now available in several sizes. But machining forged-steel tools was beyond Bill's limited finances. He couldn't afford to contract for even a limited run of special pliers, so he chose a low-cost alternative to manufacture them. He begins with standard adjustable-jaw pliers and grinds away the serrations to leave an inner curve on the outer jaw. Plier jaws bend tiny tapered prongs around the inner curve until prong tips bear firmly onto a gemstone with a tip curl. Pliers apply no force on the stone itself. Bill's expense for tools—$40 for a motor-driven two-spindle grinder. He buys standard pliers from suppliers in small quantities of two to three dozen at a time at wholesale. Grinding one pair depends on plier size but averages less than five minutes each.

No single avenue affords a proved track for successfully marketing craft tools, equipment, materials, and supplies. Two factors appear important:

❖ Craftsmen must possess a strong business sense in addition to their craft expertise plus an innovative or inventive streak.

❖ They follow a multiple-route approach to marketing using mail-order, retail store, and dealers and/or distributors. The multiple-route approach follows into promotion, advertising, and publicity with an ability to write about their products. Without these collateral abilities, the inventive craftsman may profit more by turning over the development and marketing of his or her ideas to others in exchange for a royalty.

Chapter 11

FINDING MONEY TO DEVELOP YOUR

CRAFT BUSINESS

MONEY! The need for it arises at some point in the life of every business. The amount needed may be relatively small or enormous. Telephone companies, for example, see no end to their need for new funds to finance expansion. A craft business, on the other hand, may need funds to expand production, open a shop, or to invest in accounts receivable on a much more modest scale. Generally, craft businesses tend to be "labor intensive." That is, a major chunk of the final price accounts for labor. Utilities and chemical industries, in contrast, are "capital intensive."

Businesses borrow or invest money for expansion to increase gross sales and net income. Expansion and growth represent a cult among businesses where the concept of "grow or bust" usually prevails. Money in business is used to make more money in either of two ways —to expand total volume or to cut unit costs. If you borrow money to open a shop for teaching more students than you now accommodate in your home, capital enables you to increase business potential. If you borrow money to buy a jewelry casting machine, then you are using capital to decrease unit costs.

Money, yours or others', amounts to only one form of capital. Other resources can build capital too—talent, craft know-how, and time. However, in this chapter, capital refers mainly to money or some in-kind equivalent. In-kind contributions of time and effort by an associate in exchange for some deferred compensation, barter of printing in exchange for your craft product, or sales time at a shop or exhibition in exchange for use of a shop's facilities are typical in-kind equivalents.

Capital typically comes from a variety of sources: savings, specifically yours, retained earnings from your business, cash and in-kind investments by others, and loans. You can exploit all of these sources of capital. Cash or in-kind investments will often be restricted to a partnership or corporation if the investor expects to gain a return related to the success of the business. In a partnership, for example, a person or organization may invest funds and share business profits without actively participating in the business. An investor may buy shares of stock in a corporation organized to carry on and expand a craft business without active participation.

Two kinds of capital may be used separately or together. Equity capital includes any money you or anyone else puts into the business plus retained earnings. No contract or agreement calls for repayment of equity investments except on dissolution of the business. Earnings on equity vary according to the success or failure of the business. Loans or notes are borrowed capital. Earnings on borrowed capital are paid as interest. Further, borrowed capital must be repaid according to the terms of the note or other agreement. Many craft businesses operate only on equity. Your decision to borrow money hinges on whether the added capital will earn more than it costs. Borrowing may also be necessary to keep a business going during early stages. When the business begins earning a profit, the loan is paid off.

Suppose you are operating a small craft shop out of your basement as a part-time activity. You may be teaching classes away from your home for a fee. You also sell your crafts locally and by mail through shops on consignment. You fully understand your costs, have investigated a potential market for more of your products, and recognize the steps needed to move from a part-time operation into your own full-time business. But you need a shop where you can merchandise your own products, teach students in your own facilities, and stock supplies and tools for sale to students and other craftsworkers.

You believe that borrowing the cash to open your craft shop and expand your business into a full-time operation will enable you to increase income and offer interested residents of your community better service. The sticker—where and how to borrow the cash! Before borrowing the cash, draw up a plan along the lines suggested later in this chapter. Sales projections, increased cost of operating from rented facilities, the split of your time between producing and teaching are critical points to consider. But even more important is the question—will the cash you borrow earn more than it costs in interest?

Suppose you find from a detailed analysis that you will need $5,000 in cash to rent a shop, redecorate it for teaching and selling, add a sign of some kind, invest in a suitable stock of materials, tools, and equipment for sale, and equip a number of benches for teaching. You find that, to obtain a loan of $5,000, you will be paying 12 per cent interest—$120/$1,000 or $600 per year to rent capital. If the increased business from your shop will net more than $600/year after allowances for rent and other increased operating costs from the new location, borrowing the money will pay off. Actually, your plan should project a net double or triple the actual interest to allow for unforeseen contingencies or possible miscalculations in sales or costs.

Along with paying regular interest, any plan for borrowing money should include a loan repayment schedule. Continuing to use borrowed money as part of business capital involves the concept of leverage (see below). But for small businesses, a plan for expansion financed by borrowed money should include provisions for paying off the loan over some reasonable period—one, two, or possibly up to five years. A portion of the earnings from the business will be diverted to the lender. When the loan is paid off, your equity or ownership interest in the business will have increased. During the time you are paying off the loan, the income you can draw from the business for personal spending will decrease. In effect, you are investing more equity in your business by foregoing immediate income.

Many large businesses, particularly capital-intensive businesses such as utilities, use borrowed capital regularly with little intention of ever paying off the indebtedness completely. Old loans are simply repaid with new loans. These businesses gain the advantages of leverage. Borrowed money adequately covered with mortgages on land, buildings, and equipment costs less in interest than dividends or payouts for equity capital. Such financial leverage permits a business to earn a return on borrowed money as well as on its business operations.

You may be able to apply the principle of leverage in financing your craft business, but you should be aware of the pitfalls. Suppose your small shop earns a net before tax return of 15 per cent. You will know these figures precisely if you maintain good accounts. A shop that consistently earns money will experience little difficulty in borrowing funds for expansion from a bank. If bank money costs 12 per cent interest, you would gain a spread of 3 percentage points between the cost of borrowed funds and your net earnings. On this basis, you would be better off to borrow money than to invest your own funds.

Leverage works in reverse too. If your craft business should not do as well after expansion as before and earns only 5 per cent net before taxes on a larger volume, borrowed money will increase your costs and thereby decrease your profits.

Interest on loans is fully deductible as a business expense in the year it is paid—a further advantage of using debt rather than invested equity. Earnings on equity are taxed directly if the business is organized as a corporation and again as dividends on your individual income tax return. If your business is a sole proprietorship, you pay taxes on earnings only once.

Cost of Money

Interest paid on borrowed funds is a highly visible cost of business capital. Costs of funds from alternative sources may be less visible or more difficult to calculate, but the costs may also be more onerous. For example, the side effects from a belt-tightening program to squeeze family living expenses in order to finance a business expansion may lead to emotional problems at home.

Money costs for financing may be less of a problem than non-money costs. For example, the disruption caused by bringing in an active partner or controls placed on an operation by a bank or other source of funds may sap hours from a day that can no longer be used for craft production. Therefore, both the tangible and intangible costs of money should be weighed carefully before deciding on a specific financing plan.

Before choosing which way to go, develop a written plan that outlines the options open to you for financing. Both money and intangible costs should be spelled out in your plan to avoid surprises and to afford a detailed look at all aspects. Borrowed funds, for example, will likely cost more from one source than another depending on collateral offered and the risk factor assessed by the banker or other lender. Your previous business experience and credit rating affect either your ability to get a loan or the interest rate—or both.

Interest on a loan backed by savings on deposit, negotiable securities such as stock certificates of companies listed on one of the major exchanges, or the cash value of an insurance policy will cost least— about 2¼ per cent over the rate of interest being paid on savings accounts for a passbook loan or 3 to 4 per cent over the prime rate in effect at the time for negotiable collateral loans. You may be able to borrow directly from an insurance company for a lower rate, possibly as low as 4 per cent if that rate is specified in your policy. Insurance loans are easy to get up to the cash value of your policy.

Interest on a loan backed by inventory, real estate, or accounts receivable will carry a higher rate than a loan on negotiable collateral depending on a number of factors—prime rate in effect at the time of your loan, your credit rating, value of the collateral and how quickly the collateral might be liquidated in case of a loan default, and the earnings record of your business. More about these factors later in this chapter.

Pricing the cost of equity financing where you, in effect, sell a piece of the business is more difficult to figure. A partner who may or may not actively participate in business operations will expect to share earnings rather than be paid a fixed rate of interest. If your business prospers, a percentage of the earnings could easily exceed interest on a similar amount of borrowed cash. If you incorporate your business, stockholders will expect a dividend when business is good. Payments for financing in kind—use of shop space in exchange for lessons or merchandise, printing and publicity in exchange for deferred payment in cash, and similar deals often cost more in the long run than a straight loan or investment of cash. Only by writing all of these possibilities down on separate sheets of paper and comparing benefits and associated costs can you realistically find the alternative that best suits your situation.

Invest Your Own Capital

Craft businesses reflect the talent and personal application of the owner-operator more than most small businesses. Your business is essentially you along with your artistic and production capabilities. Because of the personal nature of your business, establish it first without seeking outside financing. Bootstrap yourself into a full-time craft business by starting small, preferably in a part-time, moonlighting operation, and expanding in small secure steps.

Your interest in crafts may have started as a hobby. You acquired tools, equipment, and a backlog of materials because you were interested in developing craft skills for the fun of it. As you learn and become more proficient, you begin to give some of your craft products to friends. They, in turn, begin to buy your crafts for gifts or to use for themselves. During this phase, you spend evenings and weekends at your bench. You learn from other craftsmen in your field by buying books, attending classes, or visiting specialists. The money you spend for tools, equipment, and materials is diverted from your earnings at a separate, full-time vocation. You are investing in yourself and your craft at this stage.

As you gain proficiency and experience you may continue to expand on a part-time basis. By operating from a shop in space set aside in your own home, you save the cost of separate facilities and your overhead costs remain low. To gain experience in pricing and selling your crafts, you may enter competitions or shows to gain a reputation for yourself. You can set up shop as an "artist in action" at one of the weekend arts and craft fairs in your community. Or you can begin to place some of your products for sale on consignment in one or more local galleries or shops. During this development period, you can build up your shop's equipment, stock of materials, and variety of products for sale by plowing back earnings from your craft sales. By continuing to work at a full-time job, you need not draw out earnings from your craft business to pay for day-to-day living expenses. Continuing to turn over profits from craft sales into more materials will build your own capital—cash you have reinvested in yourself and your growing business.

Moonlighting affords you the opportunity to learn from your mistakes—in pricing, selling, promotion, and producing—at low cost. When a regular job pays for the groceries, you can risk trying new ideas and new avenues for sales. You can afford to spend time crafting entries for shows and competitions to build a reputation that will pay off later. As your part-time craft business begins generating cash, divert it into a savings account to finance later expansion. Moonlighting also develops your business acumen for planning, keeping accurate accounts, learning about taxes, and evaluating alternative marketing approaches.

At some point in your plan for becoming an independent producing-selling craftsman, you will step from a part-timer to a full-timer. Your apprenticeship while moonlighting will give you the confidence you need—plus your own funds to invest in your own new business. Financing your own business from retained earnings is the low-risk, conservative approach used by successful craftsmen and many others. "Operation Bootstrap" has been used by generations of craftsmen, usually from necessity. Few outsiders will share your enthusiasm, so you have little choice but to develop your own capital—by investing in yourself.

Capital is accumulated by saving. As you learn the business during evenings and weekends, moonlighting at shows, arts and crafts fairs, selling through the mail, you also accumulate earnings. Instead of spending these earnings, plan to plow them back into your business. Some cash will go into increased material stock and inventory. But plan to set aside cash for use in expanding your business later when times and conditions are right.

When you are willing and able to invest your own cash in a business expansion, a banker or friends with extra cash to invest will more likely listen. Therefore, as part of your long-range plan, set a goal for accumulating cash of your own. In addition to setting aside earnings from your part-time craft activities, save part of the salary or wages you now earn from your regular job. Whatever the source of other funds, you will need cash in the bank when you're ready to take the big step into a full-time business of your own.

Developing a Loan Proposal

Loans may provide part of the capital you need to expand your business. Banks make loans. People loan money to friends. Other sources for loans include credit unions, insurance companies, and various organizations dedicated to helping individuals and small businesses grow and become more profitable. All of these sources exhibit one common trait—they expect their money back with interest. Unless you find a friend who wants to help out of the goodness of his heart or a philanthropist dedicated to advancing handcrafts, a lender expects to be repaid on a definite schedule. Your biggest task in arranging for a loan is to convince a potential lender that you can and will pay back the money he may loan you. You convince the lender with a specific proposal that will include all or most of these plans prepared neatly in writing and organized by subject:

Product plan—Include a full description of your craft products. If your crafts are small, take along actual samples. For larger crafts, include photos of outstanding examples from your product line. If the money is to be used to expand your product line, include photos or sketches of the new items.

Marketing plan—Include results of any market research you may have accomplished, such as trial sales of new items at an arts and crafts fair, plus records of sales by product line at various shops including your own. Define the competition in your marketing area. If you plan to sell by mail, show any results of tests already completed, reviews of similar sell-by-mail campaigns, and a statement of why this avenue offers specific sales potential. If you now employ a salesman or plan to hire a salesman, explain in detail how you will be using his services to expand your market. Sales projections of dollar volumes expected by product line should be included in tabular form for one year and five years ahead. Summaries of your sales projections will be shown as part of your financial plan (see below). Along with your sales projections, supply backup information to assure the lender that your projections can be met and are, if anything, conservative. Previous sales figures, penetration into an established market and data on the over-all size of the market add credibility to forecasts. Some marketing plans include three sales projections—expected, optimistic, and pessimistic—to develop a range of potential gross income. Unless your marketing plan is well developed, the rest of your proposal will fall flat.

Manufacturing plan—Detail your plans for producing your crafts.

Will each piece be handcrafted from start to finish, or will certain processes be completed on machines? For example, you may spend considerable hand time on shaping or modifying wax patterns for casting jewelry. A production centrifugal casting machine would then permit multiple copies from one original. If you are a potter, will your kiln accommodate numerous pieces at one firing or will your production rate be limited by kiln capacity? Some crafts, such as some types of jewelry, lend themselves to production techniques. Other crafts, such as stitchery, include only hand time. Your manufacturing plan should include detail costs of materials and alternative sources, machine rates, if any, and labor costs per piece or group. Manufacturing costs figure prominently in the cost of sales, which directly affect operating profit. Therefore, provide specific cost data to substantiate each section of your manufacturing plan. If you do not have these data available, see Chapter 12 for ideas on setting up a practical cost-accounting system to provide such facts.

Financial plan—Money lenders understand columns of figures and dollar analyses better than craft designs. Unfortunately, most craftsmen are ill equipped to develop a financial plan. If you dislike figures, barter for help from an accountant. The important elements of a financial plan include:

❖ Dollar sales volume. Derive these figures from your marketing plan. These will be gross income figures to you. If you sell on consignment, include only the net revenue you expect to receive including your costs of handling and shipping. For the financial plan, use gross numbers rather than a detailed breakout by product line.

❖ Cost of sales. Derive these figures from your accounting system (see Chapter 12). In the cost of sales you will include materials, an allowance for your own production labor (do not include an allowance for management or selling time), purchased labor, machine time, if any, and overhead. Subtracting these costs from your gross sales leaves an operating profit.

❖ Sales and administrative expense. Selling costs, such as trips to arts fairs or shows, advertising, catalogues or brochures, and the wages of a sales person are deducted from the operating profit along with such administrative expenses as your management salary, legal fees, and similar expenses not specifically related to the cost of producing goods. The remaining dollars will be your profit before taxes. Those are the dollars expected to be available for paying off loan interest.

Your financial plan should provide a number of other figures. Working capital is the amount of money active in your business, such as cash in the bank, accounts receivable, and cost or market value of your inventory. One figure a banker will look for is your current ratio—the ratio of current assets to current liabilities. If cash, accounts receivable, inventory, and any short-term notes should total $10,000 and the amount you owe for current bills (for materials, wages accrued but not paid) totals $2,000, then your current ratio is 5 to 1. Most manufacturing businesses operate with a minimum current ratio of 2 to 1.

Loan repayment provisions should be a prominent part of your financial plan. Borrowing and repaying the loan represents a two-step process for investing in your business; therefore, the funds for repayment of the loan come out of profit. Interest on the loan is chargeable to expense, as all interest is tax deductible. Cash flow should cover the regular interest payments by a factor of two or three to allow for possible business dips. Conservative accounting practices call for loan repayments to be comfortably covered by a factor of 1.5 to 2—also to allow for mistakes in estimating or failure of sales to materialize as planned.

Summarize your proposal with a short introduction, no more than one page. Your main points here are: How much money you need, why you need it, and your plans for paying it back. Even if you need only a small amount, you gain two benefits from putting your plan together. First, by simply writing down your proposal, you crystallize your own thinking and answer questions you may not have considered in detail before. Second, by developing your plan and discussing it with a friendly loan officer at your neighborhood bank, you get the benefit of his analysis of your business plan for free. The advice and counsel you receive from a knowledgeable outsider will be worth much more than the effort you spent in pulling the figures together. Just one caution—some bankers tend to be perennial pessimists. Bankers' conservatism can be carried so far that, if you listened only to these few negative thinkers, no new business would ever be started. Select your banker carefully. He should be willing to point out weaknesses in your plan, if any. But he should offer positive ideas to resolve problems. There's no law against running your proposal by more than one loan officer for analysis—one at a time, of course. If your plan is detailed and your business offers promise, you may need to see only one.

Alternative Sources of Capital

Banks offer loans, and you may qualify for a business loan if your personal credit rating substantiates your business plan. But, frankly, banks can be difficult sources to crack unless you can offer some kind of negotiable collateral—listed stocks, a car, cash-value insurance policy, or equipment. Banks are in the business of loaning money and you need not approach a loan officer hat in hand. If you have a good business proposition, you will get an audience. If you don't gain an audience, try another bank. Even if a friendly loan officer turns down your application, he may point you in the direction of some other source.

The Small Business Administration can be a source of funds either by direct loan or as a guarantor of a loan from a bank. Two problems are associated with an SBA loan—you must not have been able to acquire financing from any other source, and the red tape plus the time for untangling the red tape can wear away even the most patient applicant at times. Nevertheless, the SBA maintains seventy-eight field offices that provide counseling and the potential of a loan. You will need to bare your financial soul to gain access to SBA direct or guaranteed loans. Counseling and advice will cost you nothing but time, so call a field office near you and sit down with one of the staffers for a session on financing. Take your proposal along to speed up the interview and provide facts.

Friends, relatives, business associates, and people you may know with money can often be talked into investing their cash in you or your business. If your business is incorporated, you may offer these people a piece of the action through an equity interest either in a straight stock sale or as an equity "kicker" along with a loan. Most states permit small businesses to sell a limited amount of stock to a limited group without a public disclosure. The number of stockholders may be limited to ten or twenty-five. Beyond that a state's equivalent of the Securities and Exchange Commission requires the development of a prospectus written to their specifications to assure complete disclosure. Ask your lawyer or a friendly banker for a reading on your state's limitations of stock sale. Less cumbersome are loans, preferably personal notes from each individual. You sign a note to pay back the loaned money at the end of a period or in installments. Personal notes can be tailored after the loans you might negotiate from a bank and will carry an agreed rate of interest. Fig. 7

Fig. 7: Typical Note For Personal Loans

Date _____

_____ (City or town)   (state)

I _____ (your name) _____ promise to pay to the order of _____ (name of person loaning money) _____ at

_____ (address) _____

_____ (number of dollars, written out) _____ _____ days after date for value received, with interest until paid at the rate of _____ per cent per annum payable in lawful money of the United States. In case suit is instituted to collect the same or any portion thereof, I agree to pay such additional sums as the court may adjudge reasonable as attorney's fees in such suit.

_____
(Your signature)

shows a sample note that may be typed with the blanks filled in to suit your case.

When soliciting funds from friends or other individuals, recognize the advantages of the "little from many" approach. That is, you will find it easier to raise $1,000 from ten people, each loaning you $100 than to get the $1,000 from one individual.

Begin your personal loan campaign by listing your friends, relatives, or others by name along with an estimate of how much you might touch them for. The more names you can add to the list, the better. Not every one on your list will come through, but you won't know until you ask them. Your reputation as a craftsman, the thoroughness of your proposal, and your personal credit standing in the community will affect your success in raising funds through personal solicitation. Many craftsmen find this person-to-person approach as the best method for growing in planned steps. A first round of financing may support a modest expansion. When these loans are paid off on schedule and your business prospers, you are in a better position to solicit a second round of personal loans. Performance in one stage builds confidence that you can and will carry through with your plan.

Small Business Investment Corporations (SBIC), Minority Enterprise Small Business Investment Corporations (MESBIC), and similar local organizations formed to finance high-risk beginning businesses may offer equity or loan capital. Your friendly banker or a counselor at the Small Business Administration will point you toward such organizations in your community. Two items will be important in dealing with such high-risk sources of capital. First, you must have established some track record. You cannot expect one of the sources to finance you from the beginning. A profitable moonlighting operation with facts organized into a business plan can be enough to build confidence that you can deliver. Second, your operation must offer a growing profit potential through growth. Here is where a detailed proposal pays off. Based on what you may have already accomplished, your proposal will show an investment analyst the benefits to be gained from investing in your business.

One caution should be observed in dealing with SBIC or MESBIC—you may pay too much for your money! That is, in exchange for a modest amount of cash, you may be asked to turn over a majority interest in your business. When this happens, you lose control.

Depending on how much cash you need, other opportunities for raising capital include supplier credit, advances from dealers or a distributor organization, and leasing of equipment. These devices amount to a deferral of payments which allows you to gain income from current production without tying up funds in advance.

Fitting all of these pieces together into a neat package that will impress a banker or other potential lender enough to lend you money calls for an over-all plan developed step by step. As an example of a typical situation distilled from several individual situations, consider the case of a jeweler we will call Charles Bitner.

Charles Bitner decided to move from being a moonlighting jeweler designing and handcrafting his own unique jewelry, into a full-time business when his firm announced he was being promoted out of New England. He and his family had learned to love the woods and the nearby skiing. He faced a full-scale family rebellion when he told about plans for moving to the hot flatlands of the middle South. So, he took stock. His reputation as a creative jeweler was well established through his appearances in local crafts fairs and competitions. His products sold regularly through a number of little galleries in the area, and his one-man shows drew patrons to galleries and generated sales. He knew he could sell his production. But could he finance a full-time business? Before refusing to move, he and Ellen, his wife, drew up a set of plans.

First, he inventoried his capital of materials, work in progress, and equipment. At a fair market value, his metal supplies, raw stones, imported gems, and findings totaled nearly $20,000—a surprising figure when he added all the pieces together. Charlie figured he could produce at least $100,000 worth of jewelry at consignment value from his stock of materials over several years. His bench tools, powered equipment, centrifugal casting machine, burnout oven, and other equipment were valued at just under $1,000 after depreciation, ample for his own use but not nearly enough to set up benches for teaching. His finished jewelry inventory, mostly out on consignment, was valued at his cost of $2,600 and amounted to fifty-nine individual pieces.

Using his accumulated capital as a start, he and Ellen worked out the financial needs for setting up a combination classroom and shop. They scouted an area dotted with boutiques and interior design studios. Already, two art galleries and a stitchery-yarn shop had located in the neighborhood. The storefront they located rented for

FINDING MONEY TO DEVELOP YOUR CRAFT BUSINESS   181

$160/month and offered enough space for eight benches for individual teaching plus space for materials and equipment. Windows and a front counter would sell Charlie's original jewelry along with student products when they were ready. They would name their shop and classroom Discovery House.

With the help of a friend at his company, Charles put together a proposal for opening Discovery House. The proposal is summarized in Fig. 8. The plan disclosed a need for $24,000 to refurbish the storefront, build and equip the eight teaching stations, add to his stock of teaching materials, and inventory a minimum stock of

Fig. 8: New Business Plan — Discovery House

	One Year	Five Years
Sales (Summary)		
Shop sales	$ 6,000	$ 42,000
Consignment sales	15,000	120,000
Materials	9,000	60,000
Equipment & tools	3,000	24,000
Lessons (fees)	6,000	54,000
Misc. sales (arts & crafts fairs, demonstrations, etc.)	3,000	18,000
Subtotal	$42,000	$318,000
Cost of Sales		
Wages (Charles & Ellen)	$18,000	$114,000
Wages (clerk)	0	24,000
Materials	1,000	12,000
Equipment & tools	2,300	19,000
Rent & overhead	6,000	34,000
Subtotal	$27,000	$203,000
Operating Profit	$15,000	$115,000
Selling & Administration		
Advertising	$6,000	$ 40,000
Travel expenses	1,200	6,000
Purchased services	2,400	18,000
Subtotal	$ 9,600	$ 64,000
Loan Repayment	$12,000	$ 24,000
Loan Interest	1,400	480
Shop Renovation	8,000	900
Subtotal	$21,400	$ 25,380
Net Profit (Loss)	($16,000)	$ 25,620

equipment for sale. Their own savings plus cash available from his voluntary savings plan would enable the Bitners to survive the loss envisioned during the first year.

When Charlie disclosed his plan to a friend at his local bank, he was refused a loan for the full amount. However, he was able to get a commitment for $12,000 by putting up his equipment and materials as collateral. With half of the borrowed capital he needed, Charlie approached a friend of the banker's for the additional capital. The industrialist had previously demonstrated an interest in crafts through his wife's participation in one of the local arts and crafts fairs. He agreed to loan $6,000 at the same interest rate as the bank, plus 10 per cent of the net profits for five years.

The remaining $6,000 came a little harder. To raise the needed cash from among his friends and associates, Charlie offered ten units of $500 each with the additional privilege of buying jewelry at consignment sale prices, that is, one third off the retail price. At the end of two months, the Bitners had their money. They signed a five-year lease and began renovating the shop. During the first year neither Charles or Ellen took any cash out of the business in order to meet the loan repayment schedule. By cutting back on their living expenses and deferring major expenses, they kept on their planned schedule of paying back all of the loans over a two-year period. Ellen worked in the shop to sell finished jewelry and materials. Charlie was able to exchange some pieces for help in putting together an advertising campaign to attract customers. But he was also able to build sales and attract students by promoting himself through a series of articles in local newspapers. Going was tough the first year, but volume gradually built, students continued to schedule lessons, and they passed the word to their friends. As they bought materials and equipment, this part of their business grew. By the end of the first year students were selling their work through the same channels as Charles—Discovery House plus a number of galleries and consignment shops. The Bitners took a 10 per cent agency fee for handling student work in addition to their usual retail markup for jewelry sold at Discovery House. At the end of the second year they had repaid their loans and were definitely "over the hump."

You, too, can develop your own plan for making money from your crafts.

Chapter 12

SUCCESS PLANNING FOR YOUR
CRAFT BUSINESS

Successful craft businesses, as distinguished from interesting hobbies, are built on one common base. Their owners recognize the necessity of following no-nonsense business practices—financing, accounting, tax planning, organization, production controls, and marketing. No successful business can ignore these essentials. According to Dun & Bradstreet, the chroniclers of business failures, lack of management attention and/or a gross lack of understanding of business practices account for most business failures. The second most common cause is a lack of money or access to financial resources.

If your objective is a successful, profitable craft business, either part-time or full-time, study and build a thorough working knowledge of the following business functions. You ignore or downgrade their importance only at the peril of failure.

Business Practices

Bookkeeping is an absolute must for any business. Uncle Sam's tax collector, our good friends at the IRS (Internal Revenue Service), demands records. State and local agencies will also demand regular accounting and payment of sales and business and occupation taxes. Even if you set prices, compute expenses, and juggle profits in your head, you must keep certain records to substantiate your income and costs when you file tax returns with the IRS, state, and local tax revenue agencies. Your form of business organization (see later in this chapter) affects the formality of your records, but some records you *must* keep.

Bookkeeping does other things for you too. Accounts can tell you, for example, whether you really are making a profit or not. If profit is not a primary motive for being in business, then this point may not be important. But pricing that recoups your cost of materials and little more leaves you working for sweatshop wages. Accurate accounts will let you know if your pricing schedules allow you to work merely for fun or to turn a profit. Many craftsmen fail to consider all of the cost factors in their business. Or they mix their costs with personal activities and end up asking questions like "Where does the money go?" or "Why can't I take out some cash for my time without going broke?" Others spend the money they take in without considering bills from materials suppliers. When the bills arrive, there's no cash left to pay, or they have to dig into their personal savings to pay off bills with money earned at another job. An effective accounting system helps solve such problems.

Rather than attempt to advise you how to set up a detailed accounting system, which is really beyond the scope of this chapter, consider these alternatives:

❖ Find an accounting firm in your community which specializes in bookkeeping for small businesses. Check the classified section of your telephone directory. Or ask your local banker, an accountant at your plant, or a friend for leads. An accounting service geared to small operations will set up and maintain your records for less than your time is worth. A basic economic tenet calls for each person to work at his highest and best skill. You are a specialist in your craft, so buy similar specialized help from a skilled accountant. The right outfit will charge you less than $100 per year for a service that sets up a system where you write your own checks, keep your bank balance in order, and pay estimated taxes to the IRS quarterly. At the end of the year the accounting service sorts through your transactions and prepares an annual report that includes a balance sheet and earnings statement suitable for filing with your annual income tax return. From this basic service, the price goes up according to your needs. Keeping track of employee tax withholdings and maintaining the other records that go along with payrolls, writing checks, filing monthly or quarterly returns, checking operating ratios, and providing monthly or quarterly operating statements will cost more.

The volume of your operations will determine how much accounting service you can use effectively. Contact two or three such services, explain your mode and volume of operations, and ask for recommendations and prices. If you can't sort out which system will serve you best for the least cost, go back to your banker or accountant friend and ask his advice.

❖ Barter some of your products for part-time help from a moonlighting bookkeeper if cash is short. Barter works wonders, as you can sometimes trade for the help you need for a fraction of the cost in out-of-pocket cash. Look around for an accountant in the groups you normally associate with—PTA, working committees, casual acquaintances at work, or at cocktail parties. You will be surprised at how approachable people can be when they stand to gain something from a proposed barter transaction. Explain your need for help in setting up an accounting system for your budding craft business. Offer to trade jewelry, pottery, or other products of your craft for his specialized help. He will work out a system in his spare time. Not only will you get an effective record system, you can probably pick his brains for cost-effective ideas in purchasing, tax-saving hints, and cost-cutting methods.

❖ Teach yourself or your spouse to keep your own books. Attend a night school class in bookkeeping to develop an understanding of basic accounting—what it will do, how it functions, and how to get started. Then, search through the stock of ready-made bookkeeping systems in any sizable store that sells business and office supplies. You will find several systems that simplify check writing and accumulate cost records, accounts payable, and accounts receivable plus forms for collecting data you will need to file tax returns.* But, unless you understand the principles of accounting, such ready-made systems will not satisfy your needs completely. You can profitably use more than just a minimum system.

* Dome Simplified Weekly Bookkeeping System, Dome Publishing Co., Dome Building, Providence, Rhode Island 02903
  Ideal Simplified Weekly Bookkeeping Record, The Ideal System Co., P. O. Box 1568. Augusta, Georgia 30903
  Also published by Ideal System are bookkeeping systems for specific types of business. Systems are available for Merchants, No. 3021, Manufacturers, No. 3131, and for General Business, No. 3611.

In addition to providing the data you need to file tax returns, a good accounting system not only reports whether your business is profitable, but which lines are more profitable than others, and which volume of business is likely to yield greater returns. The system also generates data you can use for better management of materials, labor, and overhead. Once you understand what good records can do for you, you will begin making decisions on the basis of facts rather than hunches or intuition. At that point you become a businessman or businesswoman.

Billing is one key practice you can't afford to neglect. Unless you sell only for cash, a sloppy billing system will allow income to dribble away.

Billing is closely related to credit, as there is no billing unless you ship products with the expectation of being paid later. Billing can be a mechanical system, but promptness is essential. You may send an invoice along with the package or send it separately. Invoices and sales tickets are vital elements of your sales records. Invoices can be simply printed as part of your stationery complement or purchased as standard forms with your name imprinted from such firms as The Drawing Board, Inc., P. O. Box 505, Dallas, Texas 75221.

Terms for payment will be stated on your invoices. To stimulate prompt payment, consider allowing a 2 per cent discount for payment within 10 days of the invoice date. Make sure the invoice arrives with at least 7 or 8 days for action. Common payment terms may be stated as "2/10, net 30," which simply means 2 per cent discount for payment within 10 days, or net within 30 days. A better way is to figure the cash discount and state it on the invoice. For example, if you bill out a $70.00 order, the cash discount of 2 per cent amounts to $1.40. A rubber stamp may be used which says "You may deduct —— if check is postmarked ———." Then write in $1.40 and a date 10 days ahead of your mailing date.

Don't allow customers to take the 2 per cent discount and pay 20 or 30 days later. Accept the payment, but bill them for the discount unfairly taken. They will pay up—and respect your head for business. A follow-up statement sent at the end of each month completes the normal billing cycle. If payment is not received within the 30-day stipulation, the account may be considered delinquent. A series of follow-up forms and dunning notices may also be obtained from The

Drawing Board, Inc., for use if accounts are not paid within 45–60 days. Keeping billing and statement records current in an accounts receivable file and collecting current and overdue accounts effectively will generate the profits your business deserves. Allowing assets to accumulate in delinquent accounts receivable can wreck an otherwise profitable operation.

Credit, as noted above, is a hazard for the unwary. While most retail sales in craft shops are handled for cash, wholesale distribution or consignment sales involve credit. Not all craft shops earn top credit ratings because of their slow turnover in goods. Retail establishments prefer to accept goods on a 30-day payment plan, sell them during the 30-day period, and pay the bill with the cash received. This cycle minimizes their cash investment. Craft goods sold in specialty or gift shops seldom turn over in 30 days on any sustained basis. Therefore, the owner, if he pays for goods bought wholesale, must come up with the cash out of his own pocket—that is, he must invest in inventory. As a result, craftsmen find that collecting accounts for goods sold can be slow—and sometimes frustrating.

Big business uses Dun & Bradstreet's credit rating system. That is, a business selling to another business on credit will check the credit rating of the buying business through the offices of Dun & Bradstreet, a service for which the company pays a fee related to size and services requested. A less expensive method is to ask the buyer directly for credit references. Then, call local firms and ask about his payment record. Most firms are quite conscious of their credit rating. If a firm is reported as "slow pay," plan to do business with it only on a cash or credit card basis. Selling your crafts and not collecting will drive you out of business sooner or later. When firms are out of town, simply write a letter asking for credit information and enclose a self-addressed, stamped envelope with a printed form for reply. A form used by a pottery firm is similar to the one in Fig. 9.

The request for information is sent to a reference on one of the new quick-message forms available from various business stationery supply firms. The quick-message forms may be printed with your name at the top and allow a space for your request, plus space at the bottom for a quick reply. Three or four copies are cemented together into a convenient package. You retain a copy and send two to the organization. The credit manager writes his note, keeps a copy for his

Fig. 9

We have been requested to extend credit through an open account to the organization noted below. They have supplied your name as a credit reference. We will very much appreciate any information on this organization's credit performance you can provide.

Name of organization _____

Address _____

City and State _____ Zip _____

Credit performance:

A self-addressed, stamped envelope is enclosed for your convenience.

_____

                                    Manager

file, and sends you your answer. New Truth-in-Lending Reporting requires suppliers of credit information to maintain records, and quick-message forms simplify the whole procedure.

One other way out of the credit jungle is now available. That is the use of the all-purpose bank credit card—Master Charge and BankAmericard being the two best-known systems. For a minimum fee, around $15 for a small shop, you can accept bank credit cards in payment for retail or wholesale sales. Local banks representing both nation-wide systems will be happy to explain the details and costs. The bank pays you immediately and bills the buyer for the purchase. The bank assumes the risk of collection from card holders. You pay for this service, however. When you turn over sales transactions for collection to the bank, the bank will discount the gross value of the tickets by 4½ to 6 per cent depending on the agreement you have made, the volume of business you do, and the dollar value of each sales ticket. Ordinarily, this deduction by the bank more than pays for itself in costs avoided and greater sales volume.

You may use one more option for local credit sales. Instead of checking a buyer's credit yourself, you may ask a local credit bureau for credit references. To gain this privilege, you must belong to the bureau and pay a fee for each call. In one city the charge for each reference checked is $1.75. The annual fee for belonging to the credit bureau is determined by the member's volume and type of business. Unless you plan to handle a considerable volume of credit business, the bank credit card system appears to offer the best compromise of service and low cost.

Consignment selling involves a different form of credit extension. The main difference between selling wholesale and consignment is that title to the goods remains in your name if you sell on consignment until the goods are sold. You simply permit a retail establishment to show your wares. When the seller makes a sale, he keeps his sales commission and sends you the remainder. You must be able to trust the consignment seller in the same way you extend credit. When your piece is sold, you must rely on the seller to send you your portion of the sales price. When you engage in consignment selling, select your outlets on the basis of their credit worthiness just as you would for wholesaling.

Cash sales at fairs, in your own studio, or at special events require only a simple sales slip to record the date, item, amount of the sale, and state sales tax collected, if any. Sales slip booklets are available at any large stationery store or by mail from Sears, Roebuck & Co., and the specialty suppliers, such as The Drawing Board, Inc. Totaling the sales slips gives you a picture of the gross sales for the day or an event and provides your bookkeeper with the necessary information to file state sales tax reports and federal income tax reports.

Make or Buy?

Decisions to make some of your own materials or to buy them will depend on your craft. Some jewelry craftsmen, for example, prefer to formulate their own wax for making models to be cast. These same craftsmen may also cast their own pieces in equipment they own and operate. Others will buy waxes formulated and sold by specialty suppliers and send their models to a commercial custom-casting specialist. These "make-or-buy" decisions differ basically from cost control measures where equipment decisions affect cash flow and profit. Make or buy decisions involve a number of essential factors, such as—

Quality Control—Craftsmen may not be able to buy services that meet their own exacting quality standards. The custom caster for sterling silver jewelry, for example, may not turn out consistent quality. Or, without understanding the specific requirements of an individual craftsman, the custom caster may not adjust his production work to individual considerations. The professional photographer, for example, can almost always make adjustments in his darkroom to get the specific results he deems important where a qualified but disinterested lab worker, not having seen the picture photographed, is at a loss to gain specific objectives. Similar conditions in slabbing gemstones, casting jewelry, or firing glazes may leave the craftsman dissatisfied. Potters, like Jane Wherrette, compound their own glazes because they cannot buy ready-made glazes in the quality or colors they need.

Cost—Craftsmen may figure they can do portions of the production cycle less expensively than a similar service can be purchased. Sometimes a hunch decision is completely wrong. Here is one area where accounting records can help. Incremental costs of purchased services may be cost effective when considering time and out-of-pocket expenses. For example, buying expensive equipment which may be used only a few hours a week could increase "make" costs over comparable "buy" costs.

Division of Labor—A craftsman is uniquely talented to design and fabricate some craft product. He should spend as much of his time at that function as possible and buy supporting services if they are available at a reasonable cost. Casting jewelry is a good example. An artist in metal and wax can creatively spend his or her time designing and crafting wax models to be cast. The actual casting adds little to the artistic merit of a creation because casting is mainly mechanical. The artist's best skill and talent are employed in carving or modifying the wax model. The artistic craftsman should make those parts no one else can make and buy those services available from a capable custom caster.

Convenience—Probably the most pressing reason that craftsmen make most of their own services is the convenience of sequencing through all parts of the job without interruption. Sending a wax model to a custom shop for casting interrupts the flow of designing, carving the wax, casting, and finishing a gold ring, for example. Even though a craftsman may spend valuable creative time at a mechanical part of the process, compression of over-all time may be worth the difference in productivity. Volume of production, scheduling, and investment in inventory need to be considered as trade-offs with convenience.

No tidy answers exist for make or buy questions. A right decision for one craftsman could be wrong for the next, even when both are working in the same craft field. Marketing approach, volume of production, type of product, craft field, and the craftsman's unique personality affect the final decision. For the purposes of this analysis, evaluate the factors noted and attempt to place a dollar figure on each. Aim to develop a system that yields you high dollar return for your time and investment plus a sense of satisfaction in your work. As a rule of thumb, plan to buy those services, parts, or materials that will cost you less than you can earn working at your own unique specialty.

Cost Controls

Cost controls are related to make or buy decisions and to over-all financial planning. In any business the basic equation for income is:

$$Income = Sales - Costs$$

You can increase your income by increasing sales while keeping costs in proportion. You can also increase income by maintaining the same sales volume while reducing costs. But you increase your income faster by doing both—increasing sales while decreasing unit costs. Here is where you sense the real impact of cost controls.

Increasing sales may be achieved by various means—advertising, hiring more sales persons, increasing product line variety, or cutting prices. But if costs increase faster than sales volume, you soon reach a point of diminishing returns. Maintaining a tight control over costs may be an even better route to higher income than an all-out, expensive drive to increase sales volume.

Before you can control costs, you must know what they are. Your records of materials costs, labor per unit of production, sales expense, and overhead will help you find the answers. A higher volume of production might reduce unit material costs by permitting you to buy at volume-discounted rates rather than the higher prices normally charged for small quantities. Overhead costs chargeable to each unit of production will almost always decrease as volume increases—up to a limiting point where no more production can be achieved without an increase in facilities. Labor costs may decrease with increasing volume, but marginal productivity of new people, training costs associated with adding labor, and less supervision over each employee may actually increase unit labor costs. A continuing record system enables you to control costs. You can't control costs until you know what they are. Depending on hunches and intuition may lead you in the wrong direction. Refer to the Job Cost Card in Chapter 3 for details on how to record costs.

Planning

Planning, finally, wraps all of these productivity considerations into one. Accounting systems allow you to relate productivity to profits. Designing and producing for specific markets, teaching as a means of reaching customers, and publication of your know-how and designs work together to help you achieve a profit from your craft. Your plan begins with a goal and follows through with the details of activities that must mesh to achieve your goal.

No well-conceived plan drops from the sky full blown. Most successful craftsmen start small, usually with limited funds. They experiment with selling methods, products, designs, production techniques, and materials, and usually make a potful of mistakes in the process. From this background, the serious craftsman, the real professional, evolves a plan and looks on the details of that plan as a succession of goals. Each goal becomes worth striving for in its own right. Included in an over-all plan are marketing goals, cost control goals expressed as costs per unit of production, subjective design improvement goals, and the most motivating goal of all—profit or income from the operation.

Starting a craft business takes time, talent, and money, not necessarily in equal proportions. Once you develop a plan and put it in writing, you begin to recognize weak elements. For example, you may be designing innovative fabrics and titillating stitchery hangings and enjoy every minute of the time you spend at these activities. But when you cross the line from an interesting hobby to a profit-oriented business, you must consider marketing. If you are weak in marketing, consider this element as an area that needs strengthening. If you neglect marketing and continue to design and craft your own creations hoping that someone will find you and buy your products on a continuing and hopefully increasing scale, stop kidding yourself. You are a hobbyist, not a professional, producing, selling craftsman. When you write out your plan and recognize marketing as the weak link in your chain toward a satisfying income from your crafts, then you are on your way. Your business plan will help you find your weaknesses. Your creative approach to every function, including marketing, will be your strength.

Business Organization

Only three forms of business organization are open to you. You can't escape placing yourself in one of the three. They are individual proprietorship, partnership, and corporation. Most craft businesses operate as an individual proprietorship. As a business grows, organizing as a corporation offers a number of advantages and a few disadvantages. Partnerships are simply dual or multiple combinations of individual proprietorships with added legal complications. Look closely at these considerations:

Proprietorship is simply you—owner and individual. You can start your business and stop it without government approval, although you must usually obtain a tax number and possibly a license. If you operate under some name other than your own, you must register that name with the state. Proprietorships are the least expensive form, as you need spend no cash for a corporation charter or a legal partnership agreement. Any profits from your business are simply taxed as your personal income, and you are personally liable for any debts of your business just as if you had charged a purchase personally. Proprietorships tend to be small because financing sources are limited.

Partnerships involve two or more persons, but you still need no formal government approval to operate unless you should set up a limited and general partnership, which is generally beyond the scope of most craft operations. For all partners' benefit, a written agreement specifying objectives, roles, and money contributions and withdrawals resolves possible conflicts before they begin. Oral agreements may be just as binding if witnessed, but they usually fail to define responsibilities effectively, hence the need for a written agreement.

Partnerships pay no income taxes directly. The partnership files an information return, and the partners pay individual income taxes on their proportional income—whether the income is actually received or not. Partnerships can grow larger than proprietorships because more people are available to contribute effort and money to build the business. One glaring deficiency exists for partnerships—any single partner is liable for the total debts of the partnership irrespective of his contribution or agreed-to share of any profits. Just as a proprietorship ends with the death of the proprietor, partnerships end with the death of any partner; therefore, longevity of a partnership can be a problem. Craft businesses that depend on the ability and talent of a single person or a partnership that depends on creative skills of several persons usually stop or undergo radical change if one of the principals dies. So, this deficiency need not be critical.

Corporations operate as if the chartered organization is a legal person for most purposes. To achieve such status, a corporation must meet strict state charter requirements, and costs escalate dramatically with the additional red tape. Corporations also pay taxes directly. Dividends paid to owners are paid from after-tax earnings of the corporation, and these dividends are subject to further income taxes on individuals' returns. Therefore, dividends paid are doubly taxed. When owners also participate in corporation operations, they may be paid a salary which is not subject to a corporation's tax, and the salary is only taxed once to the individual. In exchange for the complexity and added costs, the corporation offers limited liability for the owners and unlimited longevity and continuity of operation. An investor in a corporation may lose only as much as he invests in cash. Creditors may collect only from the corporation, not from the individual owners except when an individual owner has cosigned an obligation to obtain a loan or credit. Since corporations live separate, continuous lives of their own, the death of any principal or the sale of an individual's stock interest exerts little interference in a corporation's activities.

Other factors influencing your choice of organization deal in such areas as administration and control. As an individual proprietor, you are the "boss." You operate as you wish with a minimum of interference from outsiders. You prosper or fail according to your own decisions. In a partnership you share decision-making power with others and prosper or fail according to the group's abilities and decisions. Our constitution guarantees "all privileges and immunities" to individuals regardless of the state in which they live or do business. Corporations' freedom of action is much more restricted. As state-chartered "persons," a corporation may be limited in its activities in another state unless the corporation also complies with that state's regulations. Financing and the ability of a corporation to attract capital for initiation and expansion of a business rate as the biggest advantages of the corporation over the proprietorship and partnership.

Start right by starting small. Most craft businesses begin as part-time operations. Learn as you grow, and when the demands for your products exceed your part-time capability, then take the big step into the craft business full-time. When opportunities expand your need for capital, consider the money-raising advantages of operating as a corporation. If you decide to incorporate, consult an attorney for help in organizing, financing, and chartering the corporation to operate your business. As your business developed, you solved marketing, production, design, and personnel problems. Your over-all plan indicates the direction you can go as a corporation. Then, and only then, should you consider organizing your business as a corporation. But once you have gained experience, size, and marketing know-how, forming a corporation opens the door to a major opportunity for profit—capitalizing your business. When you set up a corporation and sell shares of stock, the cash you receive from shares sold becomes a personal capital gain. You pay taxes on that cash at about half the normal rate for earned income. Further, the remaining stock becomes more valuable because the market sets a price on shares in your company. How much each share will be worth depends more on the earning capacity of your company than any other factor.

Legal Considerations

Craft businesses, particularly small operations, function with a minimum of legal entanglements. However, there are a few that everyone must observe. The Uniform Commercial Code (UCC) governs the handling of money, credit transactions, banking, and the usual retail selling activities of all businesses. These are the services we all take for granted.

Insurance protection of various kinds draws support from specialists if you encounter some problem—from a visitor who gets a chip of pottery in her eye while visiting your shop to an accident to an employee. Or suppose you are a potter and a customer believes that she is the victim of lead poisoning as a result of your glazes. Product liability insurance protects you against such claims. A customer's custody policy protects you against a fire loss if furniture being repaired is destroyed while in your shop. Rather than attempt to detail all of the possibilities of insurance here, contact a general insurance agent that handles business policies. Ask his advice—and listen. Your business could be wiped out by a suit, whether you win or lose.

Warranty coverage of your products is not limited to a written pledge on a tag. Today's courts interpret merchantability more liberally, generally along the lines that a product should perform its function. If ovenwear pottery cracks the first time or the tenth time it is used, it has not performed its usual function. A customer could demand restitution under the implied "warrant of merchantability" that it will perform its intended function. So, don't claim your pottery is ovenproof if it isn't. Or don't claim your jewelry is sterling silver if, in fact, it is plated. If you have any doubt about your rights and your responsibilities, consult an attorney.

Taxes of all kinds pose problems for businessmen of every size. Corporations hire specialists to sort out their responsibilities. As a craftsman, you are obligated to pay income taxes on your earnings just as every other person who earns more than a minimum income. But as a businessman, you must also pay license fees to do business, a business and operations tax on gross or net income in certain states, collect and pass along to the state and/or city a tax on sales, and numerous other liabilities. City and state regulations vary widely on these taxes. So, consult an accountant or simply ask the city and county clerks in your city for help. Ask also about a source of information on tax liabilities at the state level, the one most likely to be involved in collecting sales taxes. When you sell out of state, you may have to collect sales taxes in some states, but not in others. Here's where you need specific advice because state requirements vary widely and change often.

Contracts and agreements can involve legal specifics too. For example, a contract involves consideration on the part of both parties to be binding. A contract to sell jewelry, for example, calls for you to give up something of value in exchange for something of value—consideration on both sides. However, a contract may evolve only after you offer something for sale, a buyer offers to buy, and you accept. An offer to sell something in a catalogue at a stated price is not a binding contract until someone offers to buy at that price and you accept. If your price is printed in error, you are not obligated to sell at that price until you accept an offer at that price.

Protection of designs and ideas interest innovative and creative craftsmen. Two opportunities are open—copyright and design patent. Of the two means, copyright is simpler, faster, and less costly. According to "General Information on Copyright" Circular 1 issued by the Library of Congress, craft designs may be copyrighted as "Works of art; or models or designs for works of art (Class G)." Class G copyrights may be obtained for "Published or unpublished works of artistic craftsmanship, insofar as their form, but not their mechanical or utilitarian aspects are concerned, such as artistic jewelry, enamels, glassware, and tapestries, as well as works belonging to the fine arts, such as paintings, drawings, and sculpture."

To copyright your designs, write to Register of Copyrights, Library of Congress, Washington, D.C. 20540, and ask for an application for Class G. Complete the application forms and send two prints of a photograph of the craft piece with the copyright fee to the Register of Copyrights. Currently the fee for one copyright is $6. After several months you will receive a certificate of copyright registration. Copyright protection runs for twenty-eight years originally and may be renewed for another twenty-eight years.

The copyright office makes no attempt to determine if your design is original. If some craftsman infringes on your design, you must take action. The certificate of copyright registration becomes a license to sue—nothing more. You must determine whether the cost of legal action warrants assertion of your rights. The fact that you have copyrighted a design may dissuade a potential infringer from producing copies, particularly if you threaten suit, as the infringer will incur legal expenses in defending the action.

Design patents may be awarded to inventors or originators of ". . . new, original and ornamental design for an article of manufacture. The design patent protects only the appearance of an article and not its structure or utilitarian features." In contrast to the copyright office, a design patent will be issued only after a search for "prior art" or evidence of a design close enough to be confused with the applicant's design. Once granted, a design patent may not be infringed by minor changes, although the interpretation of "minor changes" must be determined by a court if there is a conflict of opinion.

Design patent fees are $35 with the application and an issue fee that varies with the term—$10 for three and one-half years, $20 for seven years, and $30 for fourteen years. Drawings or photographs to support a design patent application must be according to Patent Office specifications. In addition to the fee schedule, patents are usually applied for and processed by attorneys or agents specializing in patent law, so count on legal costs of $150 to $300 in addition. Since design patents afford little more protection, if any, than copyrights, craftsmen should consider carefully the difference in costs before going the design patent route.

Craft designs endure for shorter periods than books, plays, musical compositions, or other works of art. Primary protection for your design ideas remains in your own ability to stay ahead of the field, to develop new and creative ideas rather than attempt to fend off copycats or haul them to court. While design infringers or copyists tag along behind, you can remain league-size strides ahead. Good business practice dictates holding off new and innovative designs until you can satisfy the market demand. General Motors, for example, doesn't display its new models until the factory is cranked up to supply the demand immediately. By the time a competitor could copy a GM design, the model year is over and people are looking for something new. As a craftsman, you don't enjoy the lead time of an auto manufacturer, but neither can you expect to keep producing the same designs year in and year out. Two other ideas will help you to protect your designs and markets for your innovative goods:

First, if you sell through galleries, consignment shops, or wholesale, keep a sharp eye for goods that appear after yours as knockoff copies or near copies at lower costs. Warn a store that handles copies of your pieces that you will not continue to sell against low-priced copyists. Most design-conscious owners of outlets appreciate the sales potential of new, innovative designs and will control the sale of copied goods. If they do not, move your goods out and sell them only where fresh design ideas are appreciated.

Second, price your goods realistically. An exceptionally high price encourages knockoffs because of the price umbrella. This doesn't mean that you should produce fresh, innovative designs for the same price as a quick-and-dirty "knockoff" craft producer. But when designs sell for high prices, potential profits tempt a knockoff craft producer to move in. Realistic prices that gain an advantage for your creative ideas without opening a new field for the quickies will pay off in the long run because there is less incentive for the outlet and the copycat craft producer to supply the demand.

Finally, recognize that business is business, whether that business is craft oriented or groceries. Management, a sense of business purpose, attention to the nitty-gritty details of bookkeeping, marketing, and cost controls plus consistent quality, on-time delivery, and—most important of all—consistent, continuing production are necessary to turn your craft talents and skills into profits. Anything less leaves you in the hobby class—interesting, possibly remunerative to some extent, but still a hobbyist. Learn the advantages of success planning to build your craft business and to make money from the skills you have spent time and money acquiring.

APPENDIX

Periodicals Interested in Craft Activities

ACC/Outlook, American Crafts Council, 44 West 53rd St., New York, NY 10019

American Artist, One Astor Plaza, New York, NY 10036

American Candlemaker, The, P. O. Box 22227, San Diego, CA 92122

American Glass Review, Ebel Doctorow Publications, Inc., 1115 Clifton Ave., Clifton, NJ 07013

American Home Crafts, 641 Lexington Ave., New York, NY 10022

Art Material Trade News, 25 W. 45th St., New York, NY 10036

Art Worker News, 32 Union Square East, New York, NY 10003

Artforum, 667 Madison Ave., New York, NY 10021

Artisan Crafts, P. O. Box 398, Libertyville, IL 60048

Artists Magazine, P. O. Box 4383, Albuquerque, NM 87106

Arts Magazine, 23 East 26th St., New York, NY 10010

Artweek, 1305 Franklin St., Oakland, CA 94612

Bead Journal, The, P. O. Box 24C47, Los Angeles, CA 90024

Better Homes and Gardens, 1716 Locust St., Des Moines, IA 50336

Ceramic Arts & Crafts, 30595 W. Eight Mile Rd., Livonia, MI 48152

Ceramic Scope, P. O. Box 48643, Los Angeles, CA 90048

Ceramics Monthly, P. O. Box 4548, Columbus, OH 43212

China, Glass & Tableware, Ebel Doctorow Publications, Inc., 1115 Clifton Ave., Clifton, NJ 07013

Craft Horizons, 43 West 53rd St., New York, NY 10019

Craft, Model & Hobby Industry, 229 West 28th St., New York, NY 10001

Crafts Report, The, 1529 East 19th St., Brooklyn, NY 11230
Crafts Annual, N. Y. State Craftsmen, P. O. Box 733, Ithaca, NY 14850
Crafts 'n Things, P. O. Box 1341, Arlington, TX 76010
Craftsman's Gallery, The, P. O. Box 645, Rockville, MD 20851
Creative Crafts, P. O. Box 700, Newton, NJ 07860

Decorating & Craft Ideas Made Easy, 1303 Foch St., Fort Worth, TX 76107

Early American Life, P. O. Box 1831, Harrisburg, PA 17105
Egg 'N You Review, The, P. O. Box 217, Saddle River, NJ 07458
Eggs-Aminer, The, P. O. Box 1158, Saugus, CA 91351

Family Circle, 488 Madison Ave., New York, NY 10022
Family Handyman, 235 East 45th St., New York, NY 10017
Fashion Accessories, 174 Fifth Ave., New York, NY 10010

Gem Creations, 565 Fifth Ave., New York, NY 10017
Gems and Gemology, 11940 San Vicente Blvd., Los Angeles, CA 90040
Gems and Minerals, 1797 Capri Ave., Mentone, CA 92359
Gift and Tableware Reporter, 1515 Broadway, New York, NY 10036
Gifts and Decorative Accessories, 51 Madison Ave., New York, NY 10010
Glass Art Magazine, P. O. Box 7527, Oakland, CA 94601
Glass Workshop, The, P. O. Box 244, Norwood, NJ 07648
Good Housekeeping, 959 Eighth Ave., New York, NY 10019
Goodfellow Newsletter, The, P. O. Box 4520A, Berkeley, CA 94704
Guide To The Craft World, P. O. Box 398, Libertyville, IL 60048

Handcrafters' News, 808 High Mountain Road, Franklyn Lakes, NJ 07417
Handcrafts Registry & Directory, P. O. Box 398, Libertyville, IL 60048
Handweaver & Craftsman, 220 Fifth Ave., New York, NY 10001
Hobbies, Lightner Publishing Corp., 1006 S. Michigan Ave., Chicago, IL 60605
Home Sewing Trade News, E-Z Maid, Inc., Publishers, 129 Broadway, Lynbrook, NY 11563

International Post, Urquhart Publications, P. O. Drawer 960, Santa Cruz, CA 95060
Interweave, 2938 N. County Road 13, Loveland, CO 80537

Jeweler's Circular-Keystone, 201 King of Prussia Rd., Radnor, PA 19089

Ladies' Home Journal, 641 Lexington Ave., New York, NY 10022
Lapidary Journal, P. O. Box 80937, San Diego, CA 92138

Make It With Leather, P. O. Box 1386, Fort Worth, TX 76101
McCall's, 230 Park Ave., New York, NY 10017
McCall's Needlework & Crafts, 230 Park Ave., New York, NY 10017
Mechanix Illustrated, 1515 Broadway, New York, NY 10036
Modern Needlecraft, 475 Fifth Ave., New York, NY 10017
Mott Miniature Workshop News, P. O. Box 5514, Fullerton, CA 92635

National Carvers Museum Review, 7825 S. Claremont Ave., Chicago,
    IL 60620
National Jeweler, 1501 Broadway, New York, NY 10036
National Sculpture Review, 75 Rockefeller Plaza, New York, NY 10019
Needlepoint News, P. O. Box 668, Evanston, IL 60204
North Light, 195 State St., West, Westport, CT 06880

Ozarks Mountaineer, The, U. S. 160, Forsyth, MO 65653

Pacific Goldsmith, Manchester Publications, 657 Mission St., San Fran-
    cisco, CA 94105
Pack-O-Fun, 14 Main St., Park Ridge, IL 60068
Parents, 52 Vanderbilt Ave., New York, NY 10017
Popular Ceramics, 6011 Santa Monica Blvd., Los Angeles, CA 90038
Popular Crafts, 7950 Deering Ave., Canoga Park, CA 91304
Popular Mechanics, 224 W. 57th St., New York, NY 10019
Popular Science, 380 Madison Ave., New York, NY 10017
Profitable Craft Merchandising, News Plaza, Peoria, IL 61601

Quilter's Newsletter, The, Box 394, Wheatridge, CO 80212

Redbook, 230 Park Ave., New York, NY 10017
Rug Hooker News & Views, Kennebunkport, ME 04046

Sew Business, 1271 Avenue of the Americas, New York, NY 10020
Shuttle, Spindle & Dyepot, 1013 Farmington Ave., West Hartford, CT
    06107
Southern Crafts and Art News, Rt. 14, Box 571, Cullman, AL 35055
Souvenirs & Novelties, 20–21 Wagaraw Rd., Fair Lawn, NJ 07410
Stained Glass, Stained Glass Association of America, 1125 Wilmington
    Ave., St. Louis, MO 63111

Sunset, Lane Magazine & Book Co., 80 Willow Rd., Menlo Park, CA 94025

Today's Art, 25 W. 45th St., New York, NY 10036
Tole Decor, 1616½ W. 11th Ave., Eugene, OR 97402
Toy and Hobby World, 124 E. 40th St., New York, NY 10016
Treasure Chest, The, 87 Lewis St., Phillipsburg, NJ 08865

Westart, P. O. Box 1396, Auburn, CA 95603
Woman's Day, 1515 Broadway, New York, NY 10036
Workbasket, 4251 Pennsylvania St., Kansas City, MO 64111
Working Craftsman, The, Box 42, Northbrook, IL 60062

Sources of Mailing Lists

Better Homes & Gardens
Meredith Direct Marketing
1716 Locust St.
Des Moines, IA 50336

Charles Crane Associates, Inc.
157 West 57th St.
New York, NY 10019

Chilton Direct Mail Co.
Radnor, PA 19089

Craft Lists,
1500 Shermer
Northbrook, IL 60062

Compilers, Inc.
225 West 34th St.
New York, NY 10001

CMC List Services, Inc.
50 South Warner Rd.
King of Prussia, PA 19406

Decorating & Craft Ideas
Tandy Corporation Marketing
    Services
2727 West Seventh St.
Ft. Worth, TX 76107

Dependable Lists, Inc.
257 Park Ave. S.
New York, NY 10010

Doubleday Mailing Lists
501 Franklin Ave.
Garden City, NY 11530

Gems & Minerals Magazine
The Kleid Company
605 Third Ave.
New York, NY 10016

Gift Buyers
Figis, Inc.
2525 Roddis Ave.
Marshfield, WI 54449

Handweaver & Craftsmen, Inc.
220 Fifth Ave.
New York, NY 10001

Hofheimer, Fritz S., Inc.
88 Third Ave.
Mineola, NY 11501

Holiday Handicrafts, Inc.
Richard K. Gilbert
Old Peterborough Rd.
Hancock, NH 03449

MRS Associates, Inc.
575 Lexington Ave.
New York, NY 10022

Names Unlimited, Inc.
183 Madison Ave.
New York, NY 10016

National Handcraft Institute
SDI
570 Taxter Rd.
Elmsford, NY 10523

Noma List Services
2544 Chamberlain Rd.
Fairlawn, OH 44313

Pack-O-Fun Craft Buyers
Clapper Publishing Co., Inc.
14 Main St.
Park Ridge, IL 60068

Peterson Publishing Co.
8490 Sunset Blvd.
Los Angeles, CA 90069

R. L. Polk & Co.
551 Fifth Ave.
New York, NY 10017
(also branches in Boston, Chicago, Cleveland, Detroit, Houston, Los Angeles, Philadelphia, Phoenix, and St. Louis)

Prescott Lists, Inc.
17 East 26th St.
New York, NY 10010

School Lists Mailings Corp.
1710 Highway 35
Oakhurst, NJ 07755

SDI
570 Taxter Rd.
Elmsford, NY 10523

Senior Citizens Unlimited
273 Columbus Ave.
Tuckahoe, NY 10707

Shopping International
Norwich, VT 05055

Spencer Gifts, Inc.
1601 Albany Ave.
Boulevard, Atlantic City, NJ
   08404

Wards, Lee Creative Crafts Center
1200 St. Charles Rd.
Elgin, IL 60120

Warshawsky & Company
1104 S. Wabash Ave.
Chicago, IL 60605

Wolf, Florence, Inc.
919 North Michigan Ave.
Chicago, IL 60611

Woodruff-Stevens & Assoc., Inc.
235 Great Neck Rd.
Great Neck, NY 11021

Of all the lists available, those compiled by the Tandy Corporation Computer Center, 2727 West Seventh St., Fort Worth, TX 76107, relate most closely with craft marketing. Four specific lists are available:

❖ Tandy Leather Company—634,000 buyers of leather and leathercraft, do-it-yourself projects, including books, tools, etc. List includes repeat buyers, youth group leaders, and teachers.

❖ American Handcrafts Company—227,000 current buyers of arts and crafts materials, books, and do-it-yourself kit projects.

❖ American Handcraft Society—12,668 current mail order buyers of handcraft project of the month.

❖ Merribee—85,000 buyers of needlecraft kits and supplies.

Major mailing list brokers offer consulting services, and direct-mail specialists operate in every city. Consult these sources of experienced information about your specific needs and costs. Small mailings (two thousand or less) can often be processed manually. For extensive mailings, machinery for affixing labels, stuffing, sealing, and sorting pay off in reduced costs. As noted in Chapter 7, large-scale mailings involve considerable cost, from $.25 to $1.00 each. Approach these sizable investments gradually by starting small and building on proved results.

Craft Organizations

Alabama Craftsmen's Council
c/o Susan McKeen, Sec'y-Treas.
427 South Perry St.
Montgomery, AL 36104

Arizona Designer-Craftsmen
Jacob B. Brookins, State Pres.
Faculty Box 6020
Northern Arizona University
Flagstaff, AZ 86001

Artisans Guild of Illinois
c/o Mrs. V. Steinhorn
605 Dundee Rd.
Glencoe, IL 60022

Artists & Crafts Guild of
  Nevada
2615 E. Charleston Blvd.
Las Vegas, NV 89104

California Artists' & Craftsmen's
  Guild
1131 State St.
Santa Barbara, CA 93101

Colorado Artist-Craftsmen
c/o Nilda Getty, President
1912 Mohawk
Fort Collins, CO 80521

Connecticut Guild of Craftsmen,
  Inc.
P. O. Box 94
Storrs, CT 06268

Craftsmen's Guild of Mississippi
P. O. Box 1341
Jackson, MS 39205

Delaware Craftsmen, Council for
c/o Mr. Kenton Poole, Chmn.
342 Paper Mill Rd.
Newark, DE 19711

Florida Craftsmen
c/o William Lindner
1290 S. W. 23rd St.
Miami, FL 33145

Hawaii Craftsmen
c/o Ruthadel Anderson
1170 Waimanu St.
Honolulu, HI 96818

Indiana Artist-Craftsmen
c/o Mrs. A. J. Haskens, Pres.
5801 N. Olney-12
Indianapolis, IN 46220

Iowa Designer Craftsmen
c/o Ms. Jean Sampel
2900 35th St.
Des Moines, IA 50310

Kansas Artist-Craftsmen Assn.
c/o Carol Harder, Pres.
Route 1, Box 94
Whitewater, KS 67154

Kentucky Guild of Artists and
Craftsmen
Box 291
Berea, KY 40403

League of New Hampshire Craftsmen
c/o Miss Merle Walker, Director
205 N. Main St.
Concord, NH 03301

Louisiana Crafts Council
Corner Camp St.
New Orleans, LA 70118

Maine Craftsmen, United
c/o Joan Acord
RFD #2
Litchfield, ME 04350

Maryland Craft Council
c/o Mrs. Monny Nitchie
2009 Indiana Head Rd.
Ruxton, MD 21204

Massachusetts Association of
Craftsmen
c/o Cyrus D. Lipsitt
9 Glen Ave.
Arlington, MA 02174

Michigan Craftsmen's Council
c/o Miss June Hauck
269 E. Breckenridge, #102
Huntington Woods, MI 48220

Minnesota Crafts Council
c/o Judy Onofrio
1105 10th St., S.W.
Rochester, MN 55901

Missouri Craftsmans Council
c/o Ed McEndarfer
601 S. Fible
Kirksville, MO 65501

Nebraska Crafts Council
c/o Pete Mitchell
Route #1
Nickerson, NE 68044

New Jersey Designer Craftsmen,
Inc.
c/o N. Jeane Hartman, Pres.
Usonia Old Oak Rd.
Mickleton, NJ 08056

New Mexico Designer-Craftsmen
224 Bryn Mawr S.E.
Albuquerque, NM 87111

New York State Craftsmen, Inc.
27 W. 53rd St.
New York, NY 10019

Ohio Arts & Crafts Guild
Box 26
Cambridge, OH 43725

Oklahoma Designer Craftsmen
c/o Mr. Frank Simons
1209 White Oak Rd.
Edmon, OK 73034

Pennsylvania Guild of Craftsmen
227 West Beaver Ave.
State College, PA 16801

Society of Vermont Craftsmen
c/o Mrs. Virginia Jones, Pres.
102 Main St.
St. Johnsbury, VT 05819

South Carolina Craftsmen
c/o Allan J. Sindler, Pres.
N. Brailsford Rd.
Camden, SC 29020

Tennessee Artist-Craftsmen Assn.
c/o Mrs. Sandra Blain
3702 Taliwa Gardens
Knoxville, TN 37920

Texas Designer Craftsmen
c/o Mrs. Susan Brown
4135 Wilgrove Ave.
Dallas, TX 75214

Virginia Crafts Council
c/o Harriet Anderson
6449 W. Langley Lane
McLean, VA 22101

West Virginia Artist & Craftsmen's
  Guild
c/o WV Arts & Crafts Division
WV Dept. of Com., State Capitol
Charleston, WV 25305

Wisconsin Designer Craftsmen
c/o James Zemba
Route 1
Oostburg, WI 53070

Centralo Crafters
P. O. Box 6125
Montgomery, AL 36106

Northeast Craftsmen's Assoc.
12712 Memorial Parkway
Huntsville, AL 35803

Grassroots Craftsmen
Box 637
Jackson, KY 41339

Boston Center Adult Ed.
5 Commonwealth
Boston, MA 02116

Boston YWCA Workshops
140 Claredon St.
Boston, MA 02116

Cambridge Center Adult Ed.
42 Brattle St.
Cambridge, MA 02138

Concord Art Assoc.
15 Lexington
Concord, MA 01742

Copley Society
158 Newbury
Boston, MA 02116

Learning Guild
Box 98
Newton Upper Falls, MA 02164

Leverett Craftsmen
Leverett, MA 01054

Lexington Crafts
130 Waltham St.
Lexington, MA 02173

Lowell Art Assoc.
243 Worthen St.
Lowell, MA 01852

Massachusetts Assoc. of Craftsmen
9 Glen Ave.
Arlington, MA 02174

N. E. Sculptors Assoc.
136 Pine Grove St.
Newton, MA 02146

Pittsfield Art League
39 Cliffwood St.
Lenox, MA 01240

Reading Soc. of Craft
8 Puritan Rd.
Reading, MA 01867

Women's Edu. & Indust. Un.
264 Boylston St.
Boston, MA 02116

Choctaw Arts & Crafts
Trebal Bldg., Box 21
Philadelphia, MS 39350

Albuquerque Handweavers
119 40th St., N.W.
Albuquerque, NM 87105

Stoney-Kill Potters
125 Old Ford Rd.
New Paltz, NY 12866

World Crafts Council
29 W. 53rd St.
New York, NY 10019

Art Crafters of YWCA
318 West Ave.
Elyria, OH 44035

Arts & Crafts Center
734 Oak St.
Columbus, OH 43205

Beaux Arts Club
480 E. Broad St.
Columbus, OH 43215

Chagrin Valley Art Assoc.
103 S. Main St.
Chagrin Falls, OH 44022

Ohio Arts & Crafts
800 Wheeling Ave.
Cambridge, OH 43725

Tile Club
130 13th St.
Toledo, OH 43624

Crafts Soc. of Portland
616 N. W. 18th Ave.
Portland, OR 97209

Foothills Art Guild
P. O. Box 365
Pendleton, SC 29670

Waccamaw Arts Guild
P. O. Box 1594
Myrtle Beach, SC 29577

Memphis Artists Assoc.
344 Grandview
Memphis, TN 38117

Sunrise Craft Assoc. Mis.
S. Ann Hughes Route 1
Sneedville, TN 37869

Upper Cumberland Craft
545 E. 20th
Cookeville, TN 38501

McLean Art Club
6214 Nelway Dr.
McLean, VA 22101

Richmond Craftsmen
P. O. Box 8594
Richmond, VA 23226

Tidewater Weavers
P. O. Box 1503
Virginia Beach, VA 23503

Virginia Handcrafts
2008 Longhorne Rd.
Lynchburg, VA 24501

Craftsmen of Chelsea Ct.
2909 N. Street, N.W.
Washington, DC 20007

Appalachian Craftsmen
424 Fourth Ave.
Huntington, WV 25701

Chandlers of the Mountain
Box 1776
St. Albans, WV 25177

Clay County Quiltscrafts
Box 455
Clay, WV 25043

Mountain Artisans
147 Summers St.
Charleston, WV 25301

Penny Hills Co-op
Box 18 Crooked Rd.
Scott Depot, WV 25560

Putnam Co. NTU Craftsmen
Court House Annex
Winfield, WV 25213

References

"Accounting Exercise for Craft Cooperative Bookkeepers," Francis P. Yager, FCS Service Report No. 122, Farmer Cooperative Service, USDA, Washington, DC 20250

"American Crafts: A Rich Heritage and a Rich Future," William R. Seymour, Program Aid 1026, Farmer Cooperative Service, USDA, Washington, DC 20250

American Crafts Guide, A directory of craft shops, galleries, museums, supply sources, and craftsmen throughout the United States. Gousha Publications, P. O. Box 6227, San Jose, CA 95150

"Bookkeeping Forms Your Co-op Needs," Francis P. Yager, FCS Information 82, Farmer Cooperative Service, USDA, Washington, DC 20250

"The Cooperative Approach to Crafts," William R. Seymour, Program Aid 1001, Farmer Cooperative Service, USDA, Washington, DC 20250

"Cooperative Development in Rural Areas," Three Success Stories, Reprint No. 391 from "News for Farmer Cooperatives," Farmer Cooperative Service, USDA, Washington, DC 20250

"Co-ops—A Tool to Improve and Market Crafts," Reprint No. 363 from "News for Farmer Cooperatives," Farmer Cooperative Service, USDA, Washington, DC 20250

Craft Shops/Galleries USA—A nationwide directory of outlets selling American crafts, compiled biennially. American Crafts Council, 44 West 53rd St., New York, NY 10019

Craft Sources, The Ultimate Catalog for Craftspeople, Paul Colin and Deborah Lippmen, 1975, M. Evans and Co., 216 East 49th St., New York, NY 10017

Encouraging American Craftsmen, Report of the Interagency Crafts

Committee, U. S. Government Printing Office, Washington, DC 20402

"Farmer Cooperative Publications," FCS Information 4, Farmer Cooperative Service, USDA, Washington, DC 20250

Gift and Art Shops, SBB No. 26, Small Business Administration, U. S. Government Printing Office, Washington, DC 20402

"Guides to Co-op Bookkeeping," Francis P. Yager, FCS Information 89, Farmer Cooperative Service, USDA, Washington, DC 20250

A Handbook and Resource Guide for New Craft Groups, 1972, Commission on Religion in Appalachia, Inc., 864 Weisgarber Road, Knoxville, TN 37914

The Handcraft Business, Reprint from Small Business Reporter, Vol. 10, No. 8, Bank of America, Dept. 3120, P. O. Box 37000, San Francisco, CA 94137

Handicrafts and Home Business, SBB No. 1, Small Business Administration, U. S. Government Printing Office, Washington, DC 20402

"How to Start a Cooperative," Irwin W. Rust, Educational Circular 18, Farmer Cooperative Service, USDA, Washington, DC 20250

"Is There a Co-op in Your Future?" C. H. Kirkman, Jr., FCS Information 81, Farmer Cooperative Service, USDA, Washington, DC 20250

"Legal Phases of Farmer Cooperatives: Sample Legal Documents," Morrison Neely, 1970, FCS Information 66, Farmer Cooperative Service, USDA, Washington, DC 20250

National Guide to Craft Supplies, Judith Glassman, 400 East 89th St., New York, NY 10028

New York Guide to Craft Supplies, Judith Glassman, 1971, Workman Publishing Co., 231 East 51st St., New York, NY 10022

"The Potential of Handcrafts as a Viable Economic Force," Office of Technical Assistance, Economic Development Administration, 52 pp. free from Office of Public Affairs, EDA, U. S. Dept. of Commerce, Washington, DC 20230

"Sample Legal Documents—Part I," (Legal Phases of Farmer Cooperatives), FCS Information 66, Farmer Cooperative Service, USDA, Washington, DC 20250

Selling by Mail Order, SBB No. 3, Small Business Administration, U. S. Government Printing Office, Washington, DC 20402

"Sources for Funding Arts and Crafts Programs," Linda Coe, Federal Council on the Arts and the Humanities, 806 15th St., N. W., Washington, DC 20506

Special Help for Small Businesses, SMA No. 74, Small Business Administration, U. S. Government Printing Office, Washington, DC 20402

The Visual Artist and the Law, Voluntary Lawyers for the Arts, Suite 1116, 36 W. 44th St., New York, NY 10036

"What Are Cooperatives?" C. H. Kirkman, Jr., FCS Information 67, Farmer Cooperative Service, USDA, Washington, DC 20250

INDEX

R

S